BREAKING THE
GLASS CEILING

BREAKING THE
GLASS CEILING

Sexism & Racism in Corporate America: The Myths, The Realities & The Solutions

BY ANTHONY STITH

Warwick Publishing
Toronto Los Angeles

We acknowledge the financial support of the Government of Canada through the Book Publishing Industry Development Program for our publishing activities.

ISBN: 1-894929-20-0

Published by Warwick Publishing Inc.
388 King Street, West, Suite 111, Toronto, ON M5V 1K2
1300 North Alexandria Avenue, Los Angeles, California 90027

Distributed by Firefly Books Ltd.
3680 Victoria Park Avenue, Willowdale, ON M2H 3K1

Other books by Anthony Stith
Creating a Career in the New Economy (forthcoming)

Cover design: Diane Farenick, mercer digital
Text design: Kimberley Young, mercer digital
Copy editor: Melinda Tate

Printed and bound in Canada.

This book is dedicated to all of God's children who have suffered the injustices of racism, discrimination, and prejudice, regardless of race, gender, or creed, and to my father and other poor souls whose spirits were broken or destroyed by these evils.

It is my sincere desire that this book will teach each of us that addressing and eliminating racism and discrimination is not a matter of choice, but a matter of survival.

MISSION STATEMENT

Human progress requires a vision and demands equal opportunity for every individual to achieve their potential.

Never allow any individual, institution or situation to deny you the this right and the right to make important contributions to your family and society.

Discover what you love, your talents and gifts, use them to create and fulfill your vision.

— *Anthony Stith*

The Greatest Tragedy in Life Is Not Death,
But Life . . . Life That Fails to Fulfill
Its Purpose and Potential
— *Myles Munroe, "Releasing Your Potential"*

We Must Learn to Live Together as Brothers
Or Perish Together as Fools.
— *Martin Luther King, Jr.*

CONTENTS

IN MEMORY OF BURDETTE ASHTON STITH
November 8, 1912 – March 2, 1980

We must never ignore racism and discrimination. Stand firm and be proud when addressing these twin evils. Do this regardless of the price you must pay, the pain you endure, and the things you will lose. Find comfort in knowing what you gain is more important than what you lose. Your rewards may be a long time coming, but they will come. Never allow others to silence you when combating these evils. Always act and speak with truth and integrity. Always strive toward your vision. Never allow anyone to destroy this vital part of you. These qualities are what make you unique and set you apart from others. They create self respect, the ability to love yourself and others.

Never allow racism and discrimination to diminish the spirit that allows you to achieve your vision. It is the human spirit that allows you to create a vision for yourself, regardless of what others think, say, or feel about you. Always understand you can never achieve a vision if you do not possess the inner strength to first create a vision for yourself. Within this important part of you are the gifts and talents which forge your success and make your life complete. This completeness gives you the freedom and confidence to share love not only with family and friends but with others who are different.

While it is true that confronting racism and discrimination is a tremendous burden to bear, it can also be a hidden source of great strength. We find this strength when we understand this burden is the source of our power. It propels us to seek success and happiness. This only happens when we learn to channel this burden into a motivating force, a vision, and a life's dream.

Father, I now understand why you gave up on life. Why your life was reduced to a single goal. The goal of just having enough strength to survive each day's devouring pain. The pain that stems from never achieving your life's ambition. I know why you buried your vision and feelings deep within your soul. I understand why the rejection and pain of racism and discrimination were too great to share with others. I understand your hopelessness and despair. I understand your shame, humiliation, and embarrassment from never having the opportunity to express your gift of words. I understand the great pain you felt because you were unable to share your writings with the world simply because your skin was black. I understand why your unfulfilled visions and talents became a source of pain that you were unable to bear.

Father, I stand at your grave and feel your rage and shame for succumbing to other people's prejudices. I feel your restless spirit's rage because you gave up. I know you gave up because you believed the burden was too great to bear. The fear and pain of rejection and failure paralyzed you. It prevented you from taking action to fulfill your dream. I sense your fury for not being able to provide financial and emotional stability for your family in the manner they deserved.

Father, I sense your fury for being manipulated into wasting your talents and life by toiling in professions far beneath your abilities and ambition. This was not due to your lack of desire. It was because we live in a world where our color predetermines our limits, not our abilities, desires, and willingness to work. Father, I watched you swallow your pride and work as a janitor in the elementary school I attended. I watched you sweep and mop floors to provide for your family. You did this although you knew people laughed at you, while others felt sorry for you. You did this although you knew you were educated, gifted, and capable of so much more.

Father, regardless of your position, your work ethics, intelligence, and wisdom still shone forth. Although you were forced to perform menial work, you knew you were capable of so much more. You found no satisfaction in your work but you always performed it to the best of your abilities. You believed if a job was worth doing, it was worth doing well. You rarely missed a day of work, were always polite, responsible, and well respected by others. You were the one that two teachers of Italian and German descent sought out to engage in stimulating conversations in their native languages. Another enjoyed speaking Latin with you. They found your conversations informative and enjoyable.

People always found it amazing that this black janitor could converse in five languages. Your writing and editorial skills became well known after you helped prepare and correct the thesis of a teacher who was working toward his masters degree. After this, other teachers who were working toward their advanced degrees came to you for assistance in writing and reviewing their theses. These same teachers enjoyed reading your writings and thought highly of them. Even though you were a janitor, your intelligence, knowledge, and wisdom were respected. These are the reasons why your co-workers, teachers, and principal always addressed you as "Mr. Stith," while they referred to each other by their first names. This was one of the few things that made you feel proud.

Father, I watched you hide your sorrow in a bottle to dull your pain and to help you make it through another day of watching your dreams fade farther away. I know you went through too many agonizing experiences because of your race. This is why you became a victim of this disease called alcoholism. Once, you shared the pain in your life with me. You explained that you were never allowed to work as a journalist or publish your books because you were black. You described how you went to job interviews. When they saw you were black they would laugh at you and would refuse to interview you. You explained how they escorted you from the building and told you "never to set foot on their premises again." This happened because you dared to apply for a white man's job.

You told me how you submitted articles and manuscripts that were accepted prior to publishers' knowing you were black. When you met with them and they saw that you were black, they told you they could not publish your writings because they did not accept colored writers. On a few occasions they would publish your writings under the condition it was done under a white author's name. You told me how you wrote articles for a short time but stopped because they rarely paid you. When they paid you, the payment was so little it was insulting.

When you demanded to be paid the amount promised, they told you your name was not on your writings and you could never prove you wrote them. You told me they laughed and said no one would believe "a nigger could write like this." You told me about your shame and fear when they said if you pursued this matter any further they would have you arrested. You shared with me how they published your book of poetry under a white author's name and you never received credit nor payment for your work. I saw how painful talking about these experiences was for you and now I understand why you rarely did.

Father, I personally experienced your pain after your death. This happened after I read two job rejection letters sent to you which were found in your personal belongings. The two letters were dated 11/17/31 and 6/27/32 and were in response to your written request for a journalist position. The letters were written by the Managing Editor of the *Newark Evening News*. The first rejection letter (September 17, 1931), stated how your ambition was to be a journalist. It stated how you spoke about the injustices of the color line. It also described the realities of race prejudice. How unjust it was and how it was beyond his control to hire you because of your race. While the second letter (June 27, 1932) from the same individual does not refer to the color line, the tone of the letter is of such a discouraging nature that future requests for a job appeared useless. Based on our conversations I know there were many more rejection letters like these which you were forced to endure because of your noble ambitions.

To be blessed with talents, to have strong ambitions and to live in a time when racism and discrimination were legal and the normal way of doing business is a terrifying thought. This terrifying thought was your reality. To speak out against discrimination then gives me great insight into your courage and the strength you showed at the early age of nineteen. I can understand your sense of despair and helplessness when I think about the difficulties you and other blacks endured because of your color.

During most of your life discrimination against blacks was legal. Hiring blacks in professional positions was not acceptable. You had no legal recourse available because you lived in a world of institutional racism. Then, it was at great risk to your life to speak out against racism. It would be 32 years later and you would be 51 years old before they passed the Civil Rights Act of 1964. This was the first time in our country that racial discrimination in employment was illegal. Today, 34 years after they passed this law, discrimination is still prevalent in our society.

I now realize how I watched you suffer in silence each day. I watched each day as the evils of discrimination devoured your mind, body, and spirit of its strength and dignity. It left you a shell of your former self. I saw the pain consume and devour your self-worth, emotions, and your spirit. What a great loss to the world. They never allowed you to share your gifts with others. The articles, books, and poems that were never written would have touched people's hearts, minds, and brought joy into their lives. We will never know what impact and contributions your writings could have had on our society. The lives they may have changed and the people they may have helped. To deny anyone the right to share their gifts and talents with the world is a tragic loss to everyone.

Forgive me father because I thought you were weak. I now understand how unfairly they stacked the odds against you. How they designed the laws, rules, and culture to break your spirit and to ensure people of color

14

never achieved their dreams. I finally understand how it made you feel and why you withdrew from your family, friends, and the world. This was no fault of yours. I now realize you were a strong black man who never deserted his family. A black man who provided for his family the best way he knew how.

You did this while always knowing you were capable of so much more. You always did your part in providing a roof over our heads, food, and clothing for your family. You rarely expressed outward love or emotions. I now understand that allowing yourself the joy of feeling your own emotions was too painful for you. The pain you hid would have overwhelmed you. You lost the ability to love yourself because your vision was never fulfilled.

I now understand and honor your pain by learning from it. I use our pain as my source of strength to fulfill "your vision" through me. I will not give up because I've seen what happens when we submit to racism and discrimination. I understand that spiritual death is forever and far worse than any temporary physical pain any individual endures. I now understand the pain. I treasure this valuable lesson you shared with me. Your vision will become a reality through me. My success will be our success. May your spirit now rest in peace. May your words, thoughts, and ideas forever live in print and inspire others through me.

Anthony Stith

FOREWORD

I write the foreword to this book from a unique perspective. I watched it evolve from a letter to senior management of a Fortune 100 company into the book you are about to read. It explained how this employer commonly practiced racism and discrimination and how these adverse conditions negatively affected minority employees and the company at large.

It provided valuable reasons why it is not in the best interest of American businesses to allow discrimination, racism, and sexism in the workplace. It also provided incentives for businesses to abandon these practices in the interest of self-preservation. Corporations, companies and institutions will learn why it is not profitable to allow these practices to exist in our culturally diverse society.

This book is essential for every institution and business library. Progressive companies should make it required reading for employees. It provides road maps on why and how employees should work together. Working in harmony toward common goals are in everyone's best interest. The information in this book shows how to do this in a way that propels employees and their companies toward happiness, success, longevity, and profitability.

Readers will also learn how the author and others took tragic discriminatory events in their lives and used them as opportunities to grow. They used these experiences to improve their lives and the lives of others. We can use these valuable stories to inspire us in times of crisis and whenever situations look hopeless. We can use this information to motivate ourselves. We must never view discrimination and racism as insurmountable obstacles.

Instead we must view them as challenges that we must never ignore. We must always address them with integrity and in a way that is in the best interest of all parties. This book shows discrimination and racism are the products of ignorance, low self-esteem, and unfounded fears. Even more important, this book shows discrimination and racism harm individuals, businesses, and the institutions that practice them more than the victims who are the targets of these acts.

As an Attorney, I know if businesses used the information they would become more productive, successful, and profitable. There would be limited need for the Department of Fair Housing and Employment and the Equal Employment Opportunity Commission and other government agencies of this nature.

If companies and individuals used the wisdom in this book, it would eliminate costly discrimination lawsuits. It would salvage the careers of valuable employees. It would also reduce the large number of companies that fail. Businesses and institutions fail because they refuse to hire and promote qualified employees because of their race or sex. They deprive themselves of the talent that success requires.

By using the philosophy in this book, most of the hate groups of today would no longer exist in our society. In essence we would live in a better world as true brothers and sisters regardless of our race or sex. We would live in the world that Almighty God planned for us.

Clayton Calhoun, Jr.,
Civil Rights Attorney

PREFACE

This book is not about creating or promoting discriminatory beliefs or ideas. This book was written as a tool to destroy them by developing awareness, knowledge, and the blueprints for success in today's workplace. This book is not about being anti-gender, anti-white, or anti-any race. It is about being anti-discriminatory.

The United States is not only losing its prominence in the international market; the quality of its domestic life is eroding as well. A major reason for this is our country's failure to properly use one of its most important assets: its people. A large segment of our population — African Americans, other minorities, and women — is being denied the opportunity to make important contributions. The workplace of America is no longer a place of hope, happiness, and opportunity, a place to achieve the American dream. It has become a battlefield where there are no winners.

America is denying this substantial segment of our population equal education, opportunities, and employment. Such discrimination hinders the growth of our country and is a cause of its most serious social problems.

Too many of the laws, policies, and attitudes that were developed in the 1930s and 1960s to address these inequities are inapplicable to our present working environment. They inadequately address social and civil rights violations that have persisted for decades. Current laws, policies, and customs, and recent Supreme Court decisions do not provide solutions to problems hampering our country's ability to succeed. These laws fail to provide equal employment and treatment of all citizens.

The counter-productive attitudes of racism and discrimination deny our country important technology, future leaders, and the ability to educate our population. This is why we have been unable to successfully compete in a global economy. If these attitudes go unchanged, America can look forward to a future more like a Third World country than the New World.

This is inevitable if our country continues to deny a vital segment of its work force the opportunity and ability to contribute. New ideas, policies, and laws must be implemented to prevent this disaster. No individual or institution can be concerned with only their self-interest; this only leads to self-destruction. We must seek ways to ensure the interests of all groups are promoted in congruence to guarantee our country's success.

As you will see from the dedication to my father, this book has a intensely personal dimension for me. A lot of the content derives from my experiences as an African-American man, so in places it speaks more directly to the African-American community, but anyone who has experienced discrimination or who cares about its effects on American society will find this book useful and revealing.

I am also strongly motivated by my religious beliefs, as will become apparent in this book. Beyond their worldly implications, I believe discrimination, racism, and sexism are evil abominations that are in direct conflict with God's will and purpose. My faith has given me the strength to carry on my fight against discrimination. I believe individuals need the support provided by religious belief when dealing with a phenomenon that is much larger than themselves. Victims need it to survive the demoralization that discrimination causes; perpetrators of discrimination, as well as those who stand idly by while others suffer, are also in desperate need of spiritual guidance.

Not every reader will share my particular religious beliefs, but I want to convey that discrimination goes beyond individuals and short-term concerns. I feel we need to understand that we all must eventually answer to a higher authority. The purpose of this book is to teach companies, organizations, and individuals, regardless of race, sex, or ethnic background, we are ordained by our various Gods to grow. We can prosper only by fulfilling our unique purpose in life. This book will show that only by eliminating discrimination and racism can we all achieve success. You can't afford not to read this book.

You will note that many of the situations and examples retold in this book are from anonymous sources. This is more than protecting the innocent; it is keeping food on their table.

It is the nature of our current economy that complainers — however valid that complaint may be — get passed by. The people who have told me their stories deserve protection from offenses of this sort — in fact, quoting them is no more offensive than using the journalistic device of the "unnamed source."

A NOTE TO WOMEN READERS
Much of what follows refers to the experience of various minorities — including African Americans — without regard to the sex of these minori-

ties. In addition, I have spent precious little time describing the conditions faced by white women — often conditions as degrading as those experienced by blacks and other minorities.

This is not out of ignorance or neglect, but rather, simply because I am male — and an African-American one at that. I do feel strongly that the patterns of discrimination — with the obvious exception of sexual harassment — employed by corporate America are addressed in this book. As such, I trust it is of value to all.

A Note to Canadian Readers

This book was written from an American perspective; laws and government agencies mentioned largely apply to the United States only. But you will find most of the content applies equally to Canada's multicultural society. There is much valuable information here for Canadians fighting discrimination in their workplaces.

Anthony Stith

INTRODUCTION

Today, people in the mainstream of society — non-minorities, usually male — may assume that discrimination based on race, colour, creed, or sex has been largely done away with in North America. After all, such discrimination is illegal, they think to themselves; if someone had a complaint, all they'd have to do is sue. And there are special programs in place to help minorities and women gain equal opportunity in employment. In fact, they may presume these programs are unnecessary now, since we're a long way from the days when women, if they could get jobs at all, were stuck in the typing pool, and blacks were confined to manual labor and domestic service jobs.

They notice minority employees in their offices in increasing numbers; they see more women in non-secretarial positions; the new "global" economy exposes them to people from many different ethnic backgrounds. It may be natural for them to assume that all's right with the corporate world.

But when they enter the executive boardroom, they could observe (if they chose to) that most of those seated around the table are white men. They may see people who went to the same university as they did, or grew up in the same part of town, or who play golf at the same club on the weekends. There may be the occasional minority or female face in the crowd — they can't quite remember their names, they've never actually spoken to them, but may remark to themselves, isn't it amazing that they've made it this far?

Let's view this world now from the perspective of a minority, male or female. They, too, may believe, when they first enter the corporate world, that discrimination is dead. Sure, they may expect to meet the occasional dinosaur with outdated attitudes, but overall, things should be different by now. After all, discrimination is illegal, and no company would want to damage their reputation with charges of racism or sexism.

Their employer may proudly advertise itself as "equal opportunity." The newly hired minority employees revel in the opportunities that were denied to their parents. They will be judged on their abilities and achievements alone, they think; by working hard they will prove their worth to the company and be compensated accordingly, with raises and promotions and respect from their colleagues. Thank goodness we're a long way from the days when minorities and women could only seek employment in certain sectors, largely in those jobs most white men didn't want. Minorities have proved themselves the equals of white men in all areas of endeavor; there is no longer any limit to what they can achieve.

But then reality hits, usually sooner than later. The ambitious find their achievements that they've worked so hard for are not accorded the same respect as those of their white male co-workers. They are inexplicably turned down for upper level positions for which their education, experience, and accomplishments should fully qualify them. They are kept out of the loop about office politics. They overhear crude comments directed at themselves or the minority to which they belong, made by people they formerly looked up to. They are not made to feel welcome at informal social gatherings of their fellow employees. They are not given due credit for their work. They consistently get stuck with all the boring, unappealing tasks in their department. All the "turkey" employees (unproductive but too expensive to fire) seem to be foisted on their division. They are denied the more lucrative accounts. They notice that all the upper level and executive positions in their organization are occupied by white men.

Those who dare to complain about the situation are not taken seriously and are eventually let go for some artificial reason. And they finally get the message: you are welcome here, as long as you accept the place we have set up for you. If you try to move beyond it, you will be cut down to size. Essentially, it's the same old message their parents received.

The very apt term for this situation is the "glass ceiling." It evokes a strong visual image of people pressing up against a window, getting a tantalizing view of a wonderful world before them, but being denied entry to it. The term also conveys the idea of invisibility — at one time discrimination was easy to see and point to. A "whites only" or "men only" sign certainly expresses prejudice clearly. Such blatant expressions of bigotry are largely gone from the corporate world, but the beliefs behind them continue to linger; they simply are not so easy to point to as they once were.

In the chapters that follow, I endeavor to make the glass ceiling visible and show how it can be shattered. This book describes the common tactics of businesses that practice such racism and bigotry. When you recognize these practices, it is reasonable to conclude that you and others are the victims of discrimination. The information in this book will provide you with the necessary knowledge to objectively determine if you are a victim of discrimination. It will also describe options available to combat and eliminate the evils of the glass ceiling from our society, both for individuals and for corporations that want to offer a truly equal opportunity work place.

Let us examine the challenges and obstacles minorities and women encounter in business and what must be done to achieve equal employment consideration. First, we will explore common discriminatory employment experiences. Then we will learn methods to determine "if" and "how" minorities become victims of discrimination in corporate America. Next, we will examine the procedures minorities and women must undergo to secure opportunities to obtain success in their careers.

Chapter One
WHAT'S GOING ON

Our nation is moving toward two societies, one black, one white — separate and unequal.

> — *The Kerner Commission, "Report of the National*
> *Advisory Commission on Civil Disorders," 1968*

Being a Negro in America means trying to smile when you want to cry. It means trying to hold on to physical life amid psychological death. It means the pain of watching your children grow up with clouds of inferiority in their mental skies. It means having your legs cut off, and then being condemned for being a cripple. It means seeing your mother and father spiritually murdered by the slings and arrows of daily exploitation, and then being hated for being an orphan.

> — *Martin Luther King, Jr.,*
> Where Do We Go from Here? Chaos or Community, *1967*

Today African Americans, other minorities, and women are confronted with the loss of employment, financial, and social advancements made during the sixties and seventies. In the eighties and nineties, it became apparent that the hard-won civil rights gains made by minorities have disintegrated. The two quotations above describe the conditions in our society as accurately today as when they were written more than a quarter of a century ago.

Conditions for African Americans in particular have not improved and in some cases have worsened. Thirty years have passed since President Lyndon B. Johnson established the Kerner Commission to determine the causes of the 1967 civil unrest and to develop solutions to prevent them from occurring again. The same problems not only still exist, they are more prevalent. Our nation is no longer moving toward two societies; it *is* two societies, one black, one white, separate and unequal. The quality of African-American life has deteriorated. Indisputable government and private-sector studies such as the Department of Labor's *The Glass Ceiling Initiative, Opportunity 2000* and *Workforce 2000* verify this.

Other studies by civil rights organizations (the National Urban League, NAACP, and others) economists, and sociologists also independently confirmed these realities. Their research shows African Americans are forced to endure deplorable conditions in their quest for equal employment and business opportunities. These circumstances denied them the chance to equally participate in economic, social, health, and educational advancements. This condition deprives large segments of the African-American population the ability to achieve better lives. They have been denied the opportunity to share in the wealth that America has provided to other races. The lack of employment for African Americans is a contributing factor in the disproportionate rate of poverty, crime, drugs, broken families, and violence in black communities.

Sociologist William Julius Wilson describes these circumstances in *Opportunity 2000*. He stated that while some minorities have made enormous gains in recent years, for millions of others, "the past three decades have been a time of regression, not progress, resulting in a growing economic schism between lower-income and higher-income black families." In a recent annual report, "The State of Black America," by the National Urban League, Dr. Robert Hill stated, "After making unprecedented strides during the 1960's, black families experienced sharp social and economic setbacks during the 1970's and 1980's." He explained this trend is continuing and will have a devastating impact on blacks by the year 2000.

African Americans in the 1990's are encountering increasingly disproportionate rates of poverty and unemployment. Problems that blacks are encountering in the 1990's are clarified when we review these facts: Dr. Robert Hill's article stated that the 1969 poverty rate for black families increased from 20 percent of the population to 30 percent by 1987. Recent 1990 census information determined 32 percent of the black population and 45 percent of black children now live below the poverty level compared with 8.8 percent for the white population and 15.9 percent for white children. The black unemployment rate was 6 percent in 1969; by 1987 this figure more than doubled to 13 percent of the population (a 117 percent increase). In contrast, the unemployment rate for the same periods for white Americans was 3.1 percent and 5.3 percent respectively (a 71 percent increase).

In *The State of Black America 1993,* John E. Jacob, President and Chief Executive Officer, National Urban League, Inc., stated,

> [B]lack unemployment was just over 14 percent in the third quarter of 1992, more than double the white race. But adding discouraged workers and part-time workers who want full-time jobs to the officially unemployed brings total joblessness in the African-American community to almost four million, or more than one of every four black workers. (p. 1)

The average annual African-American unemployment rates reported by the U.S. Department of labor for 1996 and 1997 are 10.5 percent and 10 percent per year. Average annual white unemployment rates for the same periods are 4.7 percent and 4.2 percent per year. Total average annual unemployment rates for 1996 and 1997 are 5.2 percent and 4.9 percent. While these figures show unemployment rates for blacks have stabilized at just more than double of whites, they fail to provide an accurate picture. Contrary to popular belief, unemployment rates are inexact measures of the number of people without jobs. They only measure the unemployed who are actively seeking employment (i.e., registered with unemployment offices). They exclude large numbers of discouraged blacks who have given up and withdrawn from the labor force. If they did include these people, black unemployment rates for 1996 and 1997 would show dramatic increases. As you read further, you will see these and other conditions have deteriorated for African Americans in the 1990's. They place the black race at great risk.

Other minorities and women are also victims of devastating discriminatory practices. These groups experienced advances in American business in the last 25 years, but they also experience needless inequities in opportunities and pay. Important facts concerning other minority groups and women are explored in this book. These conditions accurately examine the brutal realities of corporate America's relationship with African Americans, other minorities, and women. The future of minority employees appears bleak based on current attitudes, recent legal decisions, and trends that make it difficult to secure parity in the workplace.

If you question this statement consider this important fact. Congress acknowledged Supreme Court decisions such as Wards Cove Packing Co. V. Antonio, 490 U.S. 642 (1989) weakened the scope and effectiveness of the Civil Rights Act of 1964. More recently two Supreme Court decisions severely limited the use of affirmative action to achieve parity in the work-place. The first was *Adarand Constructors, Inc. v. Pena Secretary of Transportation* (June 1995). This Supreme Court decision requires that "all racial classifications, imposed by whatever federal, state, or local govern-mental actor, must be analyzed by a reviewing court under strict scrutiny and narrow tailoring." The second was the Supreme Court's refusal in 1997 to hear arguments against Proposition 209, which now provides all states the opportunity to eliminate affirmative action. Proposition 209 was the 1996 California initiative that was eventually passed, abolishing affirmative action in California. Legal decisions such as these limit and/or terminate minorities' and women's employment opportunities and legal recourse in cases of discriminatory practices.

All segments of our society have been affected by the work force revolu-tion. Minorities and women have unfairly experienced the greatest backlash. In the age of the disposable worker, employers used this phenomenon to cir-cumvent labor laws and the rights of minorities and women. Disposable workers are temps, part-timers and independent contractors. Less flattering names are short timers, per diem, leased and peripheral workers. They have little or no legal rights or benefits. When employers utilize disposable work-ers they are no longer burdened by anti-discriminatory laws and wrongful termination lawsuits. They can pick who they want and terminate relation-ships without cause or legal repercussions.

This problem becomes greater for minorities and women when we real-ize that General Motors and IBM are no longer the largest private employ-ers. That title goes to Manpower Inc., the world's largest temporary employ-ment agency, with more than half a million employees. In the near future its number of employees will double those of IBM and General Motors.

Today it is estimated that one third of Americans work in a disposable capacity that provides little or no protection. Disposable workers are expect-ed to exceed the number of full-time permanent employees by the turn of the century. This environment has created a new surge in sexual and racial harassment and discrimination. A *Time* article, "Disposable Workers," (3/29/93) stated: "Placement officers report client requests for blond bomb-shells or people without accents. Says one agency counselor: 'one client called and asked us not to send any black people, and we didn't. We do whatever the clients want, whether it's right or not.'"

These and other experiences make minority groups feel like failures and incapable of coping with American businesses. Typically, their dealings with corporate America have permanently eroded their confidence. This experience impairs African Americans' and other minorities' ability to earn a respectable living. This has had a devastating impact on their lives. In discussions with African Americans, other minorities, and women, they paint similar pictures. Their unfortunate stories have identical themes. They are confronted with needless barriers because of their race, sex, and other discriminatory reasons. They explain how these situations made it impossible to achieve success and happiness in their careers. These conditions prevent them from maintaining existing positions or climb the corporate ladder. These circumstances existed no matter how qualified they are, how hard they work, how much contributions they made, or how valuable their potential contributions were. Exploring this further, increasing numbers of minorities, and women are encountering discrimination. Discriminatory practices are common and acceptable practices in American businesses, despite their claims of being "Equal Opportunity Employers" and supporting affirmative action. Bigotry and racism are still normal activities in business.

Discrimination eventually affects everyone despite race, creed, sex, or religion. When corporations allow or condone prejudices against one group, they inevitably discriminate against other groups. If a corporation discriminates against African Americans, they will discriminate against Hispanics, Asians, Indians, women, sexual orientation, age, obesity, and so on.

In America there are substantial numbers of companies who have discriminatory practices and procedures deeply imbedded in their normal operations. There are also businesses in America that do not discriminate against minorities and women. They provide excellent training programs and opportunities to all employees.

Minorities and women often wonder if they are the victims of racism and bigotry. Most fail to take actions to determine if their feelings are true. This is one of life's greatest tragedies. It not only prevents minorities and women from achieving success and happiness in their careers; it allows discrimination to extend its evil backlash into their personal lives. Its influence negatively affects innocent family members who become secondary victims of discrimination and racism.

More important, when minorities and women ignore discrimination they become directly responsible for allowing a cancer to wreak havoc upon our society. When minorities fail to act, they become voluntary cultivators of a malignancy that devours the consciousness, spirit, and hopes of an important segment of our society. This provides bad examples for our children and will have a negative impact on their lives. Failure to act only perpetuates the cycle of bigotry. When non-minorities and minorities fail to address these evils they are no longer victims or innocent spectators. They become active participants, however unwillingly.

Racism or discrimination is not easy to prove. Businesses use covert actions and subtle techniques to shield their true intentions. We can still identify companies who practice racism and bigotry, the challenge is substantiating we are victims of racism and discrimination. Once this is done, the next challenge is to decide what can we do about it. Options are available to improve working conditions and opportunities for minorities. This is why this book was written. Discriminatory practices are injurious to our financial, physical and emotional well-being. Combating racism and bigotry is no longer an option or luxury we can ignore. The survival of our country depends upon each of us identifying and addressing racism and discrimination. We must take a stand and the appropriate steps to eliminate racially motivated practices in America.

Our first step is to take an objective and in-depth look at your employer. Most corporations and businesses have many minorities and women working for them. Everyone knows it is illegal to discriminate against minorities and women. However, a high percentage of minorities working for companies does not mean they are "Equal Opportunity Employers." We must look at important factors such as the types of positions they hold, salaries, length of employment, opportunities, and level of responsibilities.

Chapter Two
SUBTLE RACISM

I have learned that the subtle art of rejection used with finesse can be every bit as abusive as a punch in the face.

> — *Gordon Parks, black photographer, filmmaker, author*
> *"The Long Search for Pride,"* Life, 8/16/63

Sixty-seven years ago my father, a nineteen-year-old aspiring journalist, sought employment at a newspaper. As I describe in my memorial to him at the beginning of this book, he kept the letters he received in response to his application. In one letter the editor admits that, while he personally believes that a person should be taken on his or her merits, others did not see things that way, implying that he would not be able to hire a black man for fear of what others might think.

A minority or female job applicant would not receive such a frank response today. It would be imprudent for companies or their executives to acknowledge they support discrimination and racism. This would cause adverse publicity and have a devastating impact on company profits. It would also be the basis for legal action by governmental agencies and individuals. Job discrimination is not easy to identify or prove, unless you know how to frame it within the guidelines required by law. Most companies are too intelligent to have written, formal policies that acknowledge they discriminate against minorities. They know this could be used as evidence against them.

It is unusual now for businesses to publicly make racial remarks or engage in actions considered racially motivated. Businesses speak in cordial and friendly terms. When companies engage in discriminatory activities they do it discreetly. This conduct is seldom done blatantly. Discriminatory executives and employees never wear white hoods or sheets to work. They are well-groomed professionals in business suits or dresses. They do not look mean or evil.

In public, they act respectful, considerate, and speak cordially. They never call minority employees racially derogatory names. But while these terms are avoided in public, they are used behind closed doors. Minorities must be watchful of smiles and gestures that appear too friendly or insincere. Friendly smiles are often deceptive and detrimental when the person's heart and spirit do not support them.

Warm and friendly smiles are effective devices for shielding one's true intentions. The intentions behind smiles can be devious. Judge and trust individuals on more than friendly smiles and caring voices. Outwardly friendly appearances make it difficult to recognize, prove, and respond to discrimination. Many individuals project caring and concerned demeanors, while committing hideous acts and injustices against minorities.

As difficult as it appears, there are effective methods to address corporations and individuals who engage in these illegal and immoral activities. Learn to identify and address individuals and corporations who engage in discrimination. Use your experiences for personal growth and success in your career. Never allow them to destroy your quest for success. Discriminatory experiences with corporations inspired me to write this book.

Discriminatory decisions are made behind closed doors. These decisions prevent minorities from receiving equal opportunities. Let's review how these decisions are made. Decisions not to promote minorities and women are made prior to actual interviews. When minorities are involved, decisions are not based on qualifications or ability to perform the job. Decisions not to hire minorities are based on race or sex. Frequently, opportunities for learning and advancement are available only to selected groups within companies. African Americans and other minorities are unaware of promotions or training opportunities until after they are given to others.

Preferential Job Postings

Most companies have a policy of posting available positions. They use company bulletin boards, newsletters, job listings, and networking. Frequently, if African Americans or other minorities apply, they are not given the professional courtesy of an interview. They are told they are unqualified for positions they are qualified for. Even when individuals in management are not prejudiced and would employ or promote minorities, they may be unwilling to take the chance. They know hiring or promoting minorities is frowned upon by upper management. It will destroy their own chances for success. Because of this, they only hire non-minorities or a limited number of minorities. Often corporations avoid posting and advertising high-level positions. This is done to prevent minority employees from knowing about opportunities. These corporations only make non-minority employees aware of these jobs.

If these corporations do not have non-minority employee candidates available, they will still overlook qualified minority applicants. They look outside the company (via advertisements, or employment agencies). Minorities learn about these positions from rumors, classified advertisements or when a non-minority candidate is hired. In other cases, opportunities are denied by determining what skills and education qualified minority candidates are deficient in; a prerequisite of the job is then based on the qualifications they lack. When minorities do not lack any of the qualifications, imaginary requirements minorities do lack are made prerequisite for the position. These requirements are unnecessary to perform the job; they are merely used as justification not to hire qualified minority candidates.

Inconsistent Job Requirements

Another method of denying minorities employment or advancement is to overemphasize insignificant issues or weaknesses. Less important qualifications are overlooked when non-minorities are hired but strictly enforced for minority candidates. Routinely, non-minorities are hired who are not as qualified as minority candidates. Even non-minorities who are unable to meet minimum qualifications are hired, while inconsequential deficiencies in the minority candidate's résumé are given undue scrutiny and used as an excuse not to hire them.

Selective Grooming of Future Candidates

Promotional opportunities are also unavailable because corporations intentionally avoid grooming minorities and women for advancement. This is done by limiting their work experience and training opportunities. Companies actively select and groom new non-minority employees for advancement and intentionally preclude preparing existing qualified minority and woman employees.

Few words of encouragement or promotional opportunities are presented to minorities. They are made to feel alienated and not part of the management team. Minorities are intentionally made to feel uncomfortable and treated differently than non-minority counterparts. They are frequently passed over for promotions without explanation. If they bring this to management's attention, minorities are made to feel they have a problem for thinking this way. A common response is, "you are the only one who feels that way." Other explanations are invalid or make no sense. These companies may have many minority or female employees, but they only ever achieve low-level management positions, if they receive promotions at all.

Deliberate Neglect

African Americans and other minorities who reach middle management usually find it impossible to advance further. Their non-minority counterparts are usually paid higher salaries, even when they have equal or less experience and education. White male employees find advancement opportunities available to them while minority co-workers do not. Corporations who practice discrimination in such ways generally have large turnovers of African Americans and other minorities. These employees find their work conditions intolerable. They leave of their own accord or are forced to resign. They become so disenchanted they seek employment elsewhere. This unfortunate situation favors businesses. Large turnovers of minorities make company statistics on affirmative action look impressive. It inflates the number of minority employees. Records are not maintained on salary comparisons by race or sex, how long minorities were employed, and why they left. No studies are done to track minority advancement opportunities, or if minority employees are treated fairly. Companies routinely use inconclusive and meaningless statistics to create the pretense of being a true equal opportunity employer. This use of meaningless statistical data is further explored later.

Many minorities become so disenchanted with corporate America they purposely avoid corporations. They do this because of negative experiences. Unfortunately, they do not realize that leaving in this manner perpetuates discrimination. When they leave without addressing these conditions, it encourages corporations to continue these illegal practices. Existing and new minority employees will experience similar problems. This vicious cycle will continue to repeat itself.

Biased Performance Appraisals and Double Standards

Another method used to deny minorities and women promotional opportunities is through biased performance appraisals. Many qualified minorities know their ratings and salary levels are determined by prejudicial beliefs. They are not based on actual work performance, abilities, and achievements. Often there is little or no real relationship between their work performance and evaluations and salary increases. These biased, negative performance evaluations are used as justifications for not promoting qualified minorities.

Biases also become apparent in the day-to-day work environment. It is common for employers to intentionally humiliate male African Americans by debasing their manhood. An African-American manager tells of the time his white female supervisor asked him if he were looking for a fight. Feeling insulted by this comment he walked away from her. She followed him and said in a loud and threatening voice, "I want to know if you are looking for a fight? I want an answer now." This was done in front of the man's co-workers. He was finally forced to tell her he did not want to fight. She then told him if he did he would lose. Although she probably did not mean an actual fist fight, belittling him in front of others was inappropriate. This black manager was six feet tall and weighed in excess of 190 pounds. His female supervisor was about five feet three and weighed about 105 pounds. He found this treatment extremely degrading and insulting to his manhood. He felt had been spoken to as if he were a slave on a plantation in the Old South. He also felt this was a case of double standards. He knew if he had challenged her to a fight he would have been fired for threatening his superior and a woman.

Failure to Address Minority Concerns

White managers often feel they are not obligated to answer questions asked by minority employees. For example, a top salesman for a major corporation was informed that all his major accounts had been reassigned. No problems were occurring with his accounts; this African American had been the company's top salesman for the last several years. His new district had no sales, commissions, or growth potential. He asked his supervisor why the profitable accounts he had established had been reassigned to a white salesman with less seniority. In fact he had helped the white salesman obtain his position and trained him.

The supervisor said they were reorganizing the department. The salesman asked what the purpose and benefit of the reorganization was. Why were they intentionally harming him? His supervisor's replied, "I do not have the time to get into a pissing contest with you." He instructed the salesman to leave his office. The salesman demanded an answer. His supervisor finally stated it was an executive decision. This answer says nothing, answers nothing, and means nothing. Unfortunately these are common responses to legitimate minority concerns. Little more than a year later the black salesman was placed on final warning for not meeting sales quotas. Two months later he was forced to resign.

"Reorganization"

Reorganization ploys are frequently used to conceal discrimination. Minorities are informed their departments are reorganizing and then their positions are eliminated or they are demoted. Positions are not really "reorganized," just switched and shuffled. Often duties do not change, and once the minority leaves the company, positions are reorganized back to their original state. One such incident happened when a black manager complained about discrimination. Within a month he was told by his supervisor that his department was being reorganized. They told him the company was revising its corporate structure and two of his departments were transferring from finance to the administration department.

The following week they demoted him and transferred his departments to two non-black employees in the same finance department. No real reorganization occurred. They just switched two of his departments to other employees in the same finance department. They humiliated the black employee, and sent an obvious message to other employees: Never complain about discrimination or you will suffer the consequences. His employer repeatedly demoralized the black employee for two years until he resigned.

Degrading Comments and Behavior

Another form of subtle racism is the insensitive manner whites speak and act toward blacks and other minorities. Even when white employees act polite or are complimentary, they are often offensive. One such incident happened to a black employee who was a Certified Public Account (CPA).

He worked temporarily for a white supervisor who was not a CPA and had less experience. The white supervisor told the black employee he was shocked because his work was almost perfect. Whites may think this is a compliment but most blacks would question the meaning behind this statement. Most minorities would believe that statement meant the white supervisor was shocked that a black employee could perform almost perfect work. Blacks find this offensive and insulting. The black employee wanted to ask the white supervisor what he meant by the statement. But he did not ask his supervisor because he felt he would interpret his question as him having a negative attitude and it would jeopardize his job.

Another example of subtle racism happened when a black partner in a large white law firm went to work before office hours. He and a young white man entered the elevator together. The black partner and the young white man got off the elevator and walked toward the office door. Suddenly the young white man blocked his way and asked if he could help him. The black partner said no and proceeded to walk around the young white man to unlock the office door. Then the young white man again blocked his path and said in a loud and unfriendly voice, "May I help you."

The black partner identified himself as a partner in the firm. The young white male, who was a new staff attorney, quickly moved out of his way. The black partner did not look out of place — he was better dressed, in an expensive suit and tie, than the young attorney. Ironically, if the black partner had dressed in overalls, carried a broom, pail and mop, no one would never question him. They would have allowed him immediate access. Such subtle racism is based on derogatory images and myths that whites perpetuate about minorities and women.

Unfortunately, few minorities are in the position of the black law partner. They lack the authority to make others treat them respectfully. Minorities are constantly subjected to subtle and not so subtle insults that make life unbearable. Instead of responding to racial insults, most blacks and minorities learn to ignore them. They believe it is in their best interest to do so.

"Think of how much a black person has to sell of himself to try to get race not to matter . . . You have to ignore the insults. You have to ignore the natural loyalties. You have to ignore your past. In a sense you have to just about deny yourself," states Sharon Collins, a sociologist at the University of Illinois. This is a daily hardship that white males never have to endure.

"Inhuman" Resources

Few employers train employees to address minority issues. Most employers are insensitive to problems minority employees encounter. Traditional places where employees go for assistance are not receptive to minority issues. The most common place employees seek assistance is the human resources department. They can be the saviors or the final executioners of minority rights. Unfortunately, they are mostly the latter. Traditionally, human resources departments accept discrimination as the normal way companies do businesses. Therefore they do nothing about it. Minorities are discouraged from bringing these kinds of problems to human resources departments.

Few human resources personnel are properly trained to handle minority complaints. Furthermore, most of them lack the authority to resolve issues fairly and properly. Their personnel often intentionally avoid discriminatory issues because they either lack concern or fear repercussions. In some instances they discriminate more than other departments. Human resources departments are generally puppets of management. They resolve problems based on management's directions. Most human resources personnel are unwilling to take on company executives who discriminate against employees. They do not want to confront or anger powerful company executives. Personnel often know employers will not support them even if they are legally and morally correct. Questions of legality and fairness have little to do with final decisions. They generally base decisions on emotions, prejudices and acts of retaliation.

For these reasons human resources departments often view minority grievance issues as taboo. If they do respond, they seek easy solutions, which are often improper. Common practices are to overlook discriminatory complaints by ignoring them or denying their existence. Minorities dread complaining to human resources. They often fear them more than the parties who did the actual discriminating. Human resources often blackball minorities who complain. When this happens complainants are unable to transfer or obtain future promotions. Experience has shown human resources departments are unwilling or unable to protect their rights, and label them as undesirable employees. Minorities feel it is professional suicide to ask human resources for assistance in problems pertaining to racism or discrimination.

It is sometimes difficult to believe that fellow workers and managers who seem friendly, fair-minded, and competent would deliberately employ means such as those described in this chapter to limit our opportunities and ability to do our best work. It is possible that the tactics described in this chapter may be used out of ignorance rather than deliberate attempts to thwart the progress of minority and women employees, but such ignorance is not excusable in a professional environment, particularly when sincere attempts to make management aware of the problem are not taken seriously. In the next chapter, we will see how such tactics are usually not isolated or atypical, but more often are part and parcel of discriminatory attitudes that are pervasive throughout an organization.

Chapter Three
CORPORATE CULTURES

America's technology has turned upon itself; its corporate form makes it the servant of profits, not the servant of human needs.

> — *Alice Embree*
> Sisterhood is Powerful, *1970*

As stated earlier, determining whether discrimination is occurring in your work place, and then proving it, can be very difficult. Just because minorities have problems with their bosses or employers does not necessarily mean they are being discriminated against. There could be personality conflicts, true deficiencies in work performance, absenteeism, and other valid work-related issues. Problems based solely on them are unrelated to discrimination, harassment, or retaliation based on race or sex. One way of knowing the difference is to determine what type of corporate culture exists at your place of employment. Does the work environment create and support an atmosphere that allows discriminatory practices to exist and flourish? Does the company turn its back on racially motivated improprieties? Or is there genuine concern for minority and woman employee issues? For employers to be guilty of discrimination, they must show biased acts against others because of race, sex, or other protected rights. This is important to understand. Be objective and fair in assessing the situation. Review past racial patterns shown by employers. Are substantial numbers of African Americans experiencing the same problems? Do they have the same complaints?

To determine if you or other minorities are victims of discrimination, review past actions and problems of your employer and minority employees. Determine if they have provided minorities equal opportunities to succeed and advance. Determine if minority employees possess appropriate skills, education, knowledge, and experience to succeed. Most important, determine if their work performance was satisfactory. Even when minority employees' work performance is unsatisfactory, the reason why must be determined. Was it because employers intentionally prevented minorities from performing or was it because of minorities' deficiencies?

Just because minorities are not performing well does not mean they are incompetent or bad employees. Excellent employees perform poorly if they are not given proper suppor and vital information, and are discriminated against. If you can verify most African Americans, minorities, and women within the company are experiencing similar discriminatory problems and the evidence proves your findings, your feelings are justified.

Next determine if discriminatory patterns are within specific divisions or whether they are widespread throughout the company. It is important to learn if discriminatory patterns are isolated to specific employees or practiced by the employer. Obtain information about the patterns and practices of a company by observing its senior management. Senior management sets the tone and direction for the patterns developed and followed by the company.

When senior management actively engages in discrimination it becomes their normal way of doing business. This pattern becomes acceptable by all levels of company management. Are minorities and women employed in middle and senior level positions? If so, are they treated as equals? Companies often have token minorities in positions. It gives the appearance of being equal opportunity employers. In reality they are not and only do this to manipulate the law.

Another important indicator to monitor is whether companies take the initiative to correct racial inequities on their own. Does your employer take a proactive approach versus a reactive approach when addressing discrimination? Is this done on a regular or periodic basis? Does your employer prevent racial problems by addressing concerns before they become major complaints? Does it appropriately punish employees for discriminatory practices?

Are racial infractions repeatedly brought to management's attention? Does management make legitimate efforts to investigate and resolve problems in an equitable way? Are minorities allowed to voice their opinions? Are they taken seriously or are they wasting time when they bring legitimate issues to management? Last but not least, does management only show real concern when the problem becomes a threat to the company or their jobs?

Does your employer develop communications with minority employees? Does it show genuine interest in the professional development of minority and woman employees? Do they actively give minorities equal opportunities for advancement?

Are African American employees made to feel the only way to obtain success is to discard their black identities? Are black employees forced to shed all characteristics, customs and mannerisms that bond them to their race to achieve success with their employers? This is equivalent to black professional genocide. This practice forces blacks to lose their identities, beliefs and feelings. When this happens, blacks are assimilated by a white culture. They begin to think and act white. They lose kinship with their race. They become tools that prevent other minorities from advancing. When blacks are unwilling to accept black professional genocide, they are labeled as having personality problems or as undesirable employees. This is a common reason minorities are prevented from advancing or are terminated. Their only offense is that they act and look differently because of their ethnic backgrounds.

Thanks for Helping Us Become a Success, We No Longer Need Your Services

Knowing the real reasons why a company hires minorities is vital. When companies are in desperate need they become color-blind and indifferent to gender. They seek the best qualified employees to provide the talent and expertise they need to survive, regardless of race or gender. This condition has provided opportunities for minorities and women. Unfortunately, problems appear once minorities help eradicate the crisis and business is secure. Once this occurs, minorities frequently find themselves in positions where their services are no longer needed. It then becomes common for minorities to be forced out of their jobs. Non-minorities replace them once the crisis is over. The truth is discriminatory employers accept minorities when they need them in crisis situations. Minorities quickly become expendable once the crises pass. Less competent non-minorities can then safely handle these positions.

Historically, minorities are the last to be hired and the first to be terminated. Finding justifications that are clever disguises to hide discrimination is easy. Many companies are "downsizing" or "right-sizing" due to automation, cost reductions, competition, reduced profits, and an assortment of other reasons. Minorities and women are often the first choice (victims) of management when they reduce their work force. The methods used to select minorities and women for termination are often unfair and discriminatory. During the process of downsizing or right-sizing many companies use this as an opportunity to start "white-sizing" their organizations. This destroys any hope of true cultural diversity in the work force.

Inequities between non-minorities and minorities relating to job termination do not just end there. When non-minorities are terminated, they are given favorable references, severance packages and other benefits to carry them over until they obtain future employment. When minorities are terminated, they are not given adequate or fair references, compatible severance packages, benefits or assistance in obtaining future employment.

Employers often hire former employees that were laid-off as temporary employees, outside consultants or as vendors. Often their pay is equal to or greater than when they were employees. These companies also refer former employees' services to other companies. But discriminatory employers do not provide these opportunities to former minority employees. Many white senior management employees are given the so-called golden parachute when they are forced to leave. This is usually a large cash sum or benefit that provides financial security. Minorities and women are almost never given this type of benefit.

Look for this important factor: Does your corporation make compromises and concessions to correct problems that have no easy solutions? Is your corporation willing to do more than just take from its employees and the community? Does your employer admit when they make mistakes? Do they take proper actions to correct and prevent problems from occurring again? Find out if your employer has numerous discriminatory internal complaints. Also find out if they have many external complaints filed with the Equal Employment Opportunity Commission (EEOC) or the Department of Fair Housing and Employment (DFHE). In Canada, check with your provincial labor relations board.

You must be honest and objective when reviewing the conditions where you work. It is the only way you can reach sound conclusions. You need to make important observations. Ask yourself relevant questions, such as the one asked in the book, *Two Nations, Black and White, Separate, Hostile, Unequal,* by Andrew Hacker:

> In most areas of employment, even after playing by the rules, you find yourself hitting a not-so-invisible ceiling. You wonder if you are simply corporate wallpaper, a protective coloration they find it prudent to display. You begin, to suspect that a 'qualification' you will always lack is white pigmentation.

These are just some patterns to look for. They are excellent indicators in determining if you are a victim of employment discrimination. Distinguish isolated incidents from normal patterns that occur. Do this before you make your conclusions. Now that we've reviewed company patterns, let's examine specific discriminatory techniques commonly used against minorities and women by corporate America and the business world.

Chapter Four

SYSTEMATICALLY SET UP FOR FAILURE

It is a great shock at the age of five or six to find that in a world of Gary Coopers you are the Indian.

— James Baldwin, writer
Speech given at Cambridge Union, 2/17/65

As long as you keep a person down, some part of you has to be down there to hold him down, so it means you cannot soar as you otherwise might.

— Marian Anderson, opera singer
Television interview, CBS, 12/30/57

Escalating numbers of minorities and women are finding it impossible to obtain reasonable success in their careers. This problem is devastating because many of them are extremely talented and highly qualified. Minorities are finding it impossible to make it to first base. Even when they hit home runs they later find employers scored them as foul balls. The rules and treatment are not the same for minority and women employees.

What makes this problem so insidious is that white employees with less talent, dedication, and ability achieve success in their careers. They often achieve success based on the work performed by blacks and other minorities. It is common practice in American businesses to deny minorities the critical ingredients that are prerequisites to success. They often deny them the kind of support that is readily available to white employees to ensure their success.

Before we continue, we must review two types of discrimination minorities and women encounter. They are "access discrimination" and "treatment discrimination." The definition and problems associated with these two types of discrimination are explained in the *Academy of Management Journal,* 1990, Vol. 33, No 1. It is a study entitled "Effects of Race on Organizational Experiences, Job Performance Evaluations and Career Outcomes," (pages 64–86). The authors were Jeffrey H. Greenhaus, Saroj Parasurman, Wayne M. Wormey and Drexel University.

The study concluded that while African Americans gained access to managerial jobs, there is great concern regarding their treatment once employed. The study termed this "treatment discrimination."

> Unlike "access discrimination" which prevents members of a subgroup of the population from entering a job or an organization, treatment discrimination occurs when subgroup members receive fewer rewards, resources, or opportunities on the job than they legitimately deserve on the basis of job related criteria. This discrimination represents a situation in which the treatment of employees is based more on subgroup membership than on merit or achievements (Levitin, Quinn, & Staines, 1971). (p. 65)

Employers hire minorities and women. This avoids the appearance of discrimination. This fulfills the "access requirements." These same employers then engage in policies of "treatment discrimination." These are subtle and difficult to verify. Businesses that discriminate against minorities have pre-planned explanations for their actions. They always define their reasons in non-discriminatory terms.

Minorities are made to feel inferior. Their abilities are needlessly questioned. They are purposely embarrassed when they approach superiors or management for support. Minorities are subjected to undue scrutiny. They are interrogated to the point that they have second thoughts about asking for support or assistance.

> "White folks seemed always to expect you to know those things which they'd done everything they could think of to prevent you from knowing."
> — Ralph Ellison, *Invisible Man*, 1947

Minorities are promised full support when given a task. They later find this to be untrue. At the slightest sign of problems they are abandoned and left on a fragile limb. When this happens, they are isolated and left to fend for themselves.

White employees are given full support. They are given personnel, cooperation, equipment, training, and adequate time to ensure success. White employees are aware minorities do not receive adequate support. They know they do not have to take minorities seriously even if they are management. They are not required to provide minorities with proper assistance because minorities have no real authority or recourse.

This guarantees a lack of respect for minorities. This undermines their authority. White employees do not take minority employees seriously. They convey these feelings throughout the corporation. This makes minorities' jobs much more difficult than those of white co-workers. They receive minimum accouterments if they receive them at all. Their recommendations or requests are overlooked or determined unfeasible merely because minorities present them. Similar requests or recommendations by non-minorities are approved. White employees are rewarded and praised for their work. White management overlooks identical work or recommendations when presented by minorities.

Frequently minorities are forced to hire or retain undesirable employees. Often these are discarded employees no one else wanted. Minorities are not allowed to obtain the best available employees. They are given no choice but to work with less desirable employees, which makes success impossible.

Salary constraints when hiring new employees commonly restrict minority managers. They are not allowed to attract or hire the most qualified employees. Minority managers are not respected as equals. They are not allowed to hire employees of their choice. Frequently management imposes restrictions on minorities' supervision of white employees. White supervisors are not subjected to these restrictions. Minority managers are commonly forced to hire employees they are uncomfortable with. White counterparts are not forced to do this. White managers are given the flexibility to hire the best candidates. They are allowed to select employees of their choice. They have the latitude to offer higher salaries and attract the best employees. These are important tools that help create success for white employees.

Minorities are kept in the dark about important matters. Critical information required to successfully perform their jobs is intentionally made unavailable to minorities.

Minorities' work standards are set higher than white employees'. When minorities submit work that is comparable to white employees' they are rated lower or unsatisfactory. Their work is often rejected as unacceptable. Work of equal or lesser quality performed by white employees is often considered exceptional.

In many situations management intentionally undermines minorities' work. This is done to restrict their promotional opportunities or to ensure their failure. This is also done to frustrate minorities and to force them to resign. When minorities do not leave of their own accord, they are terminated for unsatisfactory performance. Biased performance evaluations are frequently given to minority employees. They are not reflective of their performance. "There is considerable evidence that raters evaluate the job performance of blacks less favorable than the job performance of whites, especially when the raters are themselves white. (Kraiger & Ford, 1985)" (Greenhaus et al., p. 66). This results in limited or no additional advancement opportunities for black managers.

An article in *Black Enterprise* (March 1994), "When Downsizing Hits Home," addresses important realities about downsizing. It explains how downsizing is manipulated so that disproportional numbers of blacks lose their jobs. Discriminatory methods used to terminate blacks during downsizing are easy to conceal and execute which places employers at little risk of legal repercussions. The article in *Black Enterprise* explained one method this way: "It's easy for managers to set people up for the squeeze because all you have to do is to begin downgrading their performance appraisals. A black person going through this process wonders if it's truly a performance issue or just a color issue." The same article quotes Kenneth P. DeMeuse, Associate Professor of Management at the University of Wisconsin at Eau Claire, who has done extensive studies of downsizing. He expressed the real concerns that blacks know about performance appraisals. "If managers are slashing jobs based on so-called objective performance appraisals, that's a real problem for minorities because we know that appraisals are rarely objective."

Businesses must understand the devastating effects biased performance appraisals have on minority and female employees, companies and our society. They do not just limit or destroy minorities' and women's careers. They impede the success of companies that allow and endorse this practice. It destroys morale, creative competition, team work, trust, and loyalty, not to mention employee dedication and commitment.

Biased performance appraisals create animosities. They prevent minorities and women from performing to the best of their abilities. When this happens, it is detrimental to employers. Discriminatory appraisals shatter the lives and visions of minorities and women. They prevent important contributions from being made to companies and our society.

An African American shared the pain and anger he still experiences from an biased performance appraisal he received 15 years ago. It not only destroyed his dream of becoming a firefighter, it almost destroyed his life. It took many attempts and several years for his acceptance into the firefighter training program. His strong desire to be a firefighter made him more determined after each rejection. He continued to apply even though he knew he was repeatedly rejected because he was black. He willingly confronted artificial barriers that prevent blacks and other minorities from becoming firefighters.

Once he was accepted, he was determined to be the best firefighter in his graduating class. During his probationary training period he and a white firefighter trainee were sent to turn off the water sprinklers in a warehouse. The water sprinklers were still on the day after they put a fire out in the building. When the two men entered the second floor, the running water was up to their chests. Because of possible gas leaks and fumes, they had been instructed to wear their breathing apparatus. The electricity was out and there were no lights except from their flashlights.

The white trainee disobeyed orders and removed his breathing apparatus. Fumes overcame him and he passed out. Fortunately the black trainee sensed something was wrong when he lost sight of his partner. He doubled back and found his partner unconscious in the water. At great risk to his life, the black firefighter removed his own breathing apparatus. He used it to keep his partner alive while carrying him out of the building. The white trainee was rushed to the hospital. He was released the following day and he returned to training.

The black trainee was never given any recognition for his heroism and quick action that saved his white partner's life. This black firefighter trainee knew if he had been white he would have received commendations and recognition for his actions. The white trainee never thanked him for saving his life. The white trainee was not reprimanded or discharged by his superiors for violating safety procedures when he admitted he removed his breathing apparatus. A week later they discharged the black employee from the training program. They gave him an unsatisfactory performance appraisal. They told him that he improperly positioned his thumbs when he was placing a two-part ladder on a building during a training exercise. This was a common minor mistake made by most trainees. When supervisors observed this, they instructed trainees how to properly place their thumbs. They never gave the black trainee a warning for this infraction. They discharged no white trainees in his class for making the same mistake.

The black trainee was so distraught and bitter he considered suicide. He later became addicted to drugs and spent three years in jail. This was an individual who had previously avoided drugs, was never involved in illegal activities, and had been deeply involved in his church before this incident. It destroyed his confidence, self- esteem, and faith. He replaced these qualities with anger and bitterness. It took five years after this incident for him to turn his life around.

About 10 years later a fire started in the building where this man worked. Because of his training as a firefighter, he immediately started supervising the evacuation of the building. After evacuating the building he used a building fire hose to keep the fire from spreading until the fire department arrived. His actions saved the building and the lives of employees. One firefighter who responded to the fire was the former trainee he saved 10 years earlier.

After the fire was out the white firefighter walked up to him and shook his hand. He said, "I've been waiting 10 years to meet you again. I always wanted to thank you for saving my life. I could not thank you during the probationary training because our supervisor warned me not to speak to you after you saved my life. He told me to never let anyone know that a nigger saved a white man's life. The supervisor said if he heard that I spoke to you, thanked you, or let anyone know you saved my life I would be discharged immediately." The firefighter also told him the supervisor said, "No matter how good that nigger is I will never allow him to become a firefighter. I will never let him take a white man's job." He said the supervisor then laughed and stated, "I am going to give that nigger a negative performance evalua- tion and discharge him although he was one of the best trainees."

This story is even a greater tragedy because biased performance appraisals are not unique to this one incident. Fifteen years later they are still common. They do a tremendous disservice not just to minorities and women but to companies and our society. They prevent our society from reaching its full potential. They do this by denying an important segment of our population the opportunity to share their talents and contributions to the world. This is a great loss to us all.

Businesses use other methods to ensure minorities have little or no oppor- tunities for promotions. They fail to provide challenging opportunities, exposure to valuable information and experience. They do not allow minorities and women into the inner circle of management or provide them with networking opportunities. "Managers' careers may be enriched by sup- portive relationships with immediate supervisors" (Baird & Kram, 1983).

Such support may take the form of career guidance and information, performance feedback, and challenging work assignments that promote development. There is some indirect evidence that black managers receive relatively little career support from their supervisors. For example, Jones (1986) reported that only 15 percent of the blacks in his sample described their organization climates as supportive for black managers (Greenhaus et al.). The same study also finds that black managers generally believe they are denied critical information essential to their career development.

The same study made other important findings in relation to the treatment of black employees and their performance. They often related legitimate low performance ratings of minorities to their poor treatment, and lack of support and not their ability. "In this study, Ilgen & Youtz (1986) suggested that race differences in actual job performance may be due to pervasive differential treatment minorities experience within organizations" (Greenhaus et al., p. 68). Disparate treatment that results in fewer and less favorable opportunities for minority members with regard to sponsorship, supervisory support, job discretion, and acceptance can affect their subsequent performance in a number of ways.

After a period of time a job becomes routine — minorities are locked into their jobs indefinitely. Failing to give minority employees challenging work creates a situation where they become bored and uninterested in their work. When this happens their job becomes mundane, unfulfilling and their work diminishes. Boredom adversely affects the performance of any worker. It can turn exceptional minority employees into mediocre performers when they lack challenges and opportunities in their work. The deterioration of minorities' performance will be subsequently reflected in their performance reviews and salary levels.

Minorities' careers are often pre-designed to last for a short period of time when they are hired. This occurs when minorities are forced to stay in lower- or middle-level positions too long. The minority employee's worth diminishes to the company as time passes. Due to annual increases and related benefits (vacation, 401k, sick time, etc.) long-term employees can become liabilities to employers. This happens when the value of their contributions do not increase. Companies can hire new employees at lower salaries and provide fewer benefits, which results in large savings.

Employers often purposely create circumstances whereby minority skills become obsolete after short periods of time. They do this by failing to provide minorities with the assignments, jobs, and responsibilities that allow workers to grow and make valuable contributions to the company. Minority employees then find themselves lagging behind their white counterparts in experience and confidence. This is the direct result of their lack of exposure. As a result, minority and women employees lack the experience to handle additional responsibilities.

Closing ranks is another effective method companies use to ensure the failure of minorities. This happens when minorities complain about managers who discriminate. Management bands together to support managers accused of discriminating against minorities. The dilemma occurs when company management supports managers who are guilty of discrimination. They are unwilling to eliminate these illegal practices.

Another method used to ensure minority managers fail is character assassination. This occurs when non-minority managers fabricate malicious stories concerning minority employees. They circulate the stories throughout the company. These stories may indicate minority managers are incompetent, difficult to get along with, or can't be trusted. A black female manager was appalled when by accident she discovered her supervisor had placed a negative confidential memo in her personnel file. She had never been sent a copy nor been informed of its existence. Every time she applied for promotions or transfer her personnel file was reviewed. Prospective interviewers were shown the negative memo.

Blacks and minorities are unfairly denied consideration for promotions by this method. Even if someone was interested in promoting or hiring minorities, a memo of this nature would persuade them to change their minds. Minorities generally are not aware memos may be placed in their personnel files without their knowledge. This can occur even if they review them. In some states the laws only require companies to show employees documents in their personnel files signed by them.

Such stories and rumors make non-minority managers reluctant to work with or associate with minority managers. Few managers are willing to take the time to investigate and determine if these accusations are true or false. These are just some methods used by companies and corporations to ensure that minorities and women fail in the corporate world. Learn to recognize them. Later in this book we will explain how to address these and other problems minorities encounter.

Chapter Five
MINORITIES DISCRIMINATING AGAINST MINORITIES

Racism in its nationalist phase . . . has been a politician's plaything . . . It is a dangerous plaything, a sword which can be turned in any direction to condemn the enemy of the moment.

—Ruth Benedict
Race, Science and Politics, *1940*

What we're saying today is that you're either part of the solution or you're part of the problem.

— Eldridge Cleaver
Speech, San Francisco State
Post-Prison Writings and Speeches, *1963*

The black man who wants to turn his race white is as miserable as he who preaches hatred for the Whites.

—Frantz Fanon
Famous Black Quotations and Not So Famous, *p. 30*

Companies sometimes intentionally create atmospheres and conditions where minorities must compete against other minorities for all the wrong reasons. This happens when there are disproportionately small hiring quotas and opportunities for minorities. Corporations often indoctrinate minority employees to believe the only way they will advance and succeed in business is by discriminating against other minority employees. Often they make these employees feel they must disregard their identity to fit in and to achieve success. Black employees often refuse to associate with other black employees.

Minorities often discover the more they discriminate against fellow minorities the more they are rewarded. In some situations this indoctrination is so embedded within a company that minorities discriminate more than whites. Businesses that discriminate against minorities create this type of climate.

This condition serves as an ideal cushion or buffer if there are repercussions against the company. This method of deception insulates firms from accusations of discrimination. They simply claim they didn't do it or had no knowledge of the problems. They transfer the blame solely to minority managers.

These situations cause resentment within the minority population. They are similar to the tactics used during slavery. Plantation owners created divisions among the slaves. They created "house niggers" whom they gave preferential treatment. They taught them to look down on "field niggers." House niggers reported any activities of field niggers that slave owners disapproved of. They rewarded house niggers for spying and betraying field niggers.

During research for this book I reviewed letters from an African-American to his employer's management. They expressed legitimate concerns regarding racism and discrimination. They discussed how the company rated and treated minorities on an unequal scale. He explained how his employer deemed him incompetent after saving them millions of dollars. He was outraged they never gave him recognition for his outstanding work. The letter complained about the firm's refusal to acknowledge his excessive uncompensated overtime and how they denied him bereavement and sick leave according to company policy. In one letter he wrote,

> As a small boy, I recall my grandmother relating stories of the "Ole South" and the indignities under which Blacks were forced to live. The most poignant of these stories was what happened to black field workers at the hands of plantation owners. You see, they were paid by how much cotton (weight) they could pick in a day. If the owner was in a charitable mood, one would be paid according to the actual amount picked and the preset scale. However, if the owner did not like a certain field worker, or he had noted that field worker attempting to get ahead by buying land or sending his children to school he was punished. That field worker's daily portion of cotton would be lost, somewhere between the scale and the owner's barn. Thus the worker was not paid. If one complained, the practice would continue. If one persisted, one could be beaten and fired, or just fired. This could result in starvation for the worker and his family. Sir, it appears that little or nothing has changed in the last one hundred years.

Businesses who engage in discrimination still use similar tactics today. Instead of misplacing minorities' "cotton," they devalue or ignore minorities' successes. They overlook their accomplishments. They punish severely minorities who complain. Complaintants are used as examples to discourage others. Other minorities and non- minorities are too frightened to complain or to be supportive of others who do. Instead of physical beatings they are mentally tormented and humiliated. Complainers are fired or forced to quit. These minorities forfeit any hope of receiving positive references, which are essential to their careers.

Minority managers feel businesses frown upon them if they associate closely with other minorities at work. Even today black managers feel uncomfortable networking with other blacks and minority employees. Minorities feel uncomfortable going to lunch in groups or showing support for each other. Minorities believe if they develop close relationships with other minority employees, it will hurt their careers. This is why many African American do not to associate with each other at work. This explains why minorities develop little camaraderie among themselves. African-American employees often fear they will be chastised if they are too friendly toward their race or other minorities.

Even worse, employees often feel they will be viewed unfavorably if they hire or promote minorities and women, even if they are the most qualified candidates. Because of this dilemma, minorities discriminate against other minorities in their hiring and promotional practices. They do this because they fear offending/alienating their co-workers and superiors.

Minorities realize that there are limited numbers of managerial positions available to them. Most realize they retain their jobs only because they are the token minority or their numbers remain disproportionately small. These deplorable situations cause many minorities to resent themselves and fear minority employees. This fear prevents qualified minority managers from being mentors, and cultivating the careers of other minorities. They feel this will result in them training minorities as their replacements. For white employees this is not a problem. For them training employees as replacements is wise. It helps their chances for promotion because they have immediate replacements for their jobs. This allows them to advance quickly. White employees are not restricted by unwritten quotas.

However, this is not the same for blacks and other minority employees. Training other minorities becomes a realistic threat to minority managers.

They know their chances for advancement are limited. They also know they are vulnerable to being replaced when forced to stay in the same position too long. Instead of minorities moving up the corporate ladder, they are forced out or fired once they reach a predetermined plateau. Minorities know from experience that when they hire a new minority manager or trainee another minority manager's job is in jeopardy.

The disproportionately low number of management jobs for African Americans creates resentment among the ones who work in lower-level positions. They feel African-American managers in higher-level positions purposely shun them. Instead of working together, they are often forced to work against each other. They must do this to retain their positions and/or secure promotions. Instead of helping each other they are sabotaging each other's chances for success. Management encourages these activities. They are the primary reasons why minority employees discriminate against each other. On the other hand, white employees are free to mingle, promote, hire and associate within their race. They do this without fear of repercussions. They do not have to be concerned about backlashes from these normal activities.

Minorities are often used for discriminatory purposes without their knowledge. This happens when black or other minority employees raise issues about discrimination or try to eradicate this conduct. They often find themselves unemployed because of their anti-discrimination efforts. To protect themselves, companies intentionally hire another minority or woman as a replacement. They select minorities whom they feel will not be threats concerning issues relating to discrimination. This provides an almost perfect defense. Employers use the fact that they hired another minority or as their defense against charges of racism or sexism. When they feel the danger has passed, they sometimes terminate the new minority employee without cause.

These companies make it known that employees are to stay clear of agitators. Employees know that if they fail to do so they will suffer the same consequences. Most minorities are in such fear of reprisals they will do almost anything to prove they will not challenge discrimination. They will deny any form of racism or bigotry exists even when they know they are victims of it. To protect their jobs they will not support minorities' claims of discrimination.

These are just some of the reasons why minorities discriminate against minorities. Minorities must learn that they become willing victims when they are forced or fooled into behaving in this self-destructive manner. It is not in their long-term interest to allow others to manipulate them.

Minorities must learn the importance of unity, networking, and working to ensure all parties have equal opportunities. The importance of networking with other minorities to improve working conditions is essential for successful careers.

Chapter Six
GOING THROUGH THE MOTIONS

Words spoken without meaning have no tentacles. They float endlessly, bouncing here and there, restless pieces of the spirit; sent out without any mission or specific destination, landing no where and serving no purposes, except to diminish the spirit of the speaker.

— *J.C. Bell*
Famous Black Quotations, *p. 51*

Being a star has made it possible for me to get insulted in places where the average Negro could never hope to go and get insulted.

— *Sammy Davis, Jr.*
Yes I Can, *1965*

"Civil Rights" is a term that did not evolve out of black culture, but, rather, out of American law. As such, it is a term of limitations. It speaks only to physical possibilities — necessary and treasured, of course — but not of the spirit.

— *Alice Walker*
In Search of Our Mothers' Gardens, *1983*

When victims of discrimination approach employers they are often met with concerted efforts to discredit them and their complaints. This is done without any investigation of the complaint. In some situations management appears to be concerned and promises to thoroughly investigate the matter. Unfortunately, after a token investigation, management concludes the complaint has no merit. This frequently happens even when the facts prove minorities' complaints and concerns are valid.

Common responses from companies are similar to this one: "We reviewed employment statistical data. It clearly shows minorities comprise a large or even a majority percentage of the management." An example once given was that management consists of 34 percent African Americans, 33 percent

Hispanic and 33 percent whites. They neglect to inform you statistical interpretation is often erroneousness and misleading.

Accurate and meaningful statistics representing minority employees is important. Unfortunately it is only a small part of the equation required to eliminate discrimination. We must also look beyond statistical numbers. We must examine the realities of the working conditions minority employees endure. The following is a short list of important elements that must be evaluated with statistical analysis. Only after these factors are validated can it be used to prove equality in the work place.

1. Statistics showing percentages of minority employees without titles fail to show if minority employees equally participate in entry, middle and senior positions. Qualified minority employees are often restricted to lower-level positions. Even when minorities can obtain high-level positions they are often limited to areas of low salaries.

2. Employment statistics fail to provide time comparisons showing average times for whites and minorities to obtain managerial positions. Non-minorities may be promoted quicker through the ranks while qualified minority employees must wait years longer just to be considered for the same promotions. Statistics fail to show these invisible barriers that prevent minorities from equally progressing to higher levels.

3. These statistics fail to consider salary inequities between non-minorities and minorities. This requires comparative reviews of salaries and positions held by non-minority and minority employees. This will require comparing the two groups' educations, work experience, skills and length of employment. Minorities often have more education and experience than non-minorities but still have lower positions and salaries.

4. These statistics also provide no insight into biased performance appraisals and salary increases. There must be studies to analyze minority and non minority performance reviews, merit increases, bonuses, and other benefits. Annual performance reviews for African American and other minorities often reflect biased ratings/salary increases. They are inconsistent with their level of performance. Excellent work often results in average performance rating. Average performance results in

an unsatisfactory review. This is not only frustrating but it ensures minorities and women will not receive opportunities for advancement.

5. These statistics do analyze high turnover rates for minority employees but these figures can be used to inflate the number of minority employees. Often, terminated minorities are used to calculate current statistical data. They are left on statistical records for extended periods before being deleted. The turnover ratio for non-minorities is lower. Statistics do not show they stay because they are given more opportunity and receive higher salaries.

6. Statistics are limited in providing important information. They never reflect minorities' feelings about their jobs or employers. They fail to show whether minority employees are happy or are mistreated. They do not show if minorities are victims of discrimination. They fail to show why an employer fired or demoted minorities. They do not tell how long minorities stayed in the same position nor the number of times they were denied promotions they deserved. They fail to show the number of minorities hired as temporary employees.

7. These statistics never reflect unequal working conditions or unequal terms of employment. They never reflect minorities' fears and concerns for their jobs when they complain about discriminatory practices. They never reflect if employers are mistreating minorities and women. they do not evaluate whether minorities receive the same support in their work.

8. One final comment about statistics: They can easily be manipulated to support the outcome you desire. This is done by using a biased selection of data from the available population or selecting a biased population. We cannot determine the accuracy of statistical conclusions when we do not have access to the information used to compile them. Politicians running for office are perfect examples. Opposing candidates take independent polls which show opposite results based on their statistical sampling. Each candidate's poll shows they will win their election that they have the support. Reality is often different.

Corporations and companies who discriminate against minorities try to keep complaints secret. They isolate and terminate minorities who expose this problem. They do not include this information in their statistics (i.e., legal actions, minority complaints and their relationships to terminations). Often only after companies incur many legal actions do they start to seriously investigate minority complaints. When this happens, it is only done to protect themselves from future legal actions or adverse publicity.

Often they gather company data from questionnaires, surveys and climate assessments which they do not make public. Vital information is not used for eliminating or correcting discrimination, only to protect the status quo or for damage control. This is typical when companies prepare questionnaires that intentionally exclude questions that address or expose discriminatory activities. This is confirmed when individuals who conduct these surveys make it clear they are instructed not to discuss issues pertaining to discrimination. If discrimination data are collected, they are recorded separately from the facts used to make decisions or recommendations. Often they manipulate the outcome of these surveys and interviews. This is common when company employees conduct these surveys rather than independent groups.

When discrimination complaints are made employers often offer to find minorities other positions within the company — or they blackball these employees. This prevents them from obtaining future positions or promotions within the company. Ultimately these minorities find it impossible to properly perform their jobs. It is not due to their lack of abilities or efforts; it is because of the adverse treatment they receive. Minorities become so frustrated they leave on their own. If they do not leave of their own accord, they are asked or forced to leave. This is called constructed termination.

Constructed termination happens when the actions and conditions of a company become so intolerable it would cause any reasonable person to resign. This occurs when they treat minorities as outcasts. Fellow employees will not work with them or give them support. Other examples include making minorities work under conditions that are detrimental to their health.

Here is an example of a corporation going through the motions: An African-American manager worked for a corporation for five years. He discussed his and other minorities' concerns with his superiors and human resources. His complaints and grievances accomplished nothing. He felt that the corporation was not genuinely interested in eliminating discriminatory practices. Next he addressed his concerns in writing to the president of his organization. The letter included proper documentation and had adequate support (names, dates, incidents, witnesses, etc.). He asked for an audience to discuss his grievances.

He was a reputable employee in a responsible position and anticipated the professional courtesy of a direct reply from the president. The president did not have enough concern or interest to respond directly. There was no contact nor any effort made to meet with the employee. The president assigned the matter to the vice president of human resources. The vice president of human resources met with the employee on four or five occasions, but consistently gave him the runaround and never addressed or resolved any of the issues. Issues and meetings were intentionally dragged on for more than five months. Meetings were scheduled, canceled and rescheduled by the vice president of human resources. The company simply "forgot" the incident once they felt the employee had calmed down.

This African-American manager provided detailed accounts of discrimination within the finance department where he worked. He brought this to the human resources department's attention. The vice president of human resources and the manager of employee relations promised him they would do all they could to obtain him a position outside the finance department. But they never did assist him in finding or interviewing for any positions.

When this employee applied for a position on his own, he was rejected without even the professional courtesy of an interview. After four months of no assistance, he found himself in for a big surprise. They reorganized his department and they demoted him. This was a little more than four months after he complained of discrimination. He questioned the manager of employee relations concerning his demotion. He was told nothing could be done.

When he asked the manager about the promise to find him another position, they insulted him with this response: The manager informed him that finding a position outside the finance department was based on the 5 percent to 95 percent rule — 5 percent effort by human resources and 95 percent effort by the employee. The manager told the employee the human resources department did not have the time or staff to assist him. This corporation had had no real intention of transferring this employee. They just waited for several months to pass. This allowed the discrimination issue to cool down and to avoid the impression that the company retaliated against him because of his complaint. After a short period passed, the company began to put pressure on the employee to resign. It soon becomes apparent that many companies, like this one, have no intention of addressing discrimination problems.

Many of these same employers openly stated they support equal employment and have affirmative action programs. These companies talk about accepting cultural diversity and seeing their work force as a melting pot of all nationalities. Often their actions do not support their words. Jesse Jackson explained it this way: "I hear that melting pot stuff a lot, and all I can say is that we haven't melted" (interview, *Playboy,* 11/69).

Another concept to understand is that companies have more than the responsibility of just hiring minorities and women. Their legal and moral obligations do not end after they are hired. Businesses have a responsibility and legal obligation not to treat minorities as second-class employees. This happens when corporations clearly define restricted roles for minority employees. They do not impose these same boundaries upon white employees. These companies impose artificial boundaries that minorities are conditioned to believe they can never overcome.

Unwritten and unspoken rules which are invisible but real and made known to all employees perpetuate these boundaries. They define the limited roles which are designed for minority and women employees. Fear, unfriendly stares or gestures, retaliation and intimidation enforce these unwritten rules. When minority employees cross these boundaries, they do it at great risk to their careers. Any minority that tries to step beyond these boundaries becomes an outcast and finds him or herself unemployed or severely punished. These businesses create conditions and atmospheres where they exercise complete control over the way minority employees think and act.

Companies like these deny minority employees opportunities to function as free thinkers and the opportunity to grow as individuals. These corporations intentionally create environments where they deny minority employees opportunities to exercise free thinking, voice opinions, openly confront discriminatory and racial issues, and demonstrate their abilities. Carter G. Woodson, a pioneer in the study of black history, explains the simple and hideous reason why companies conduct businesses in this manner:

> When you control a man's thinking, you do not have to worry about his actions. You do not have to tell him not to stand here or go yonder. He will find his "proper place"

and will stay in it. You do not need to send him to the back door. He will go without being told. In fact, if there is no back door, he will cut one for his special benefit.(*Famous Black Quotations,* p. 32)

When you find these conditions and the atmosphere described in this chapter, you have valid reasons to be concerned about racism and discrimination. If they occur where you are employed do not give up hope. This book describes options you have available to address these problems. These options are effective in changing discriminatory policies and procedures. They teach corporations it is in their best interest to change and to provide minority employees equal access to success.

Chapter Seven

THE GLASS CEILING

Racism is so universal in this country, so widespread and deep-seated, that it is invisible because it is so normal.

> — *Shirley Chisholm*
> Unbrought and Unbossed, *1970*

The struggle for equal opportunity in America is the struggle for America's soul. The ugliness of bigotry stands in the direct contradiction to the very meaning of America.

> — *Hubert H. Humphrey*
> Beyond Civil Rights — A New Day of Equality, *1968*

Today minorities and women are encountering a multitude of barriers that have prevented them from obtaining entry, middle or senior positions in corporations and companies. These barriers have prevented minorities from reaching maximum earning potential and preparing for advancement opportunities in the work place. Blacks and other minorities are still feeling the symptoms of "institutional racism." For more than four hundred years institutional racism has existed in our country. It consists of written and unwritten laws, and public policy designed to discriminate against blacks and other minorities. It was known as institutional racism because it was acknowledged and openly practiced by reputable institutions, including public and private businesses, law enforcement, colleges, government officials and agencies. Though laws have been enacted to eliminate and prevent discrimination and institutional racism, bigotry and prejudice are still prevalent today. Because discrimination is illegal, it can no longer be classified as "institutional" racism and openly acknowledged as a way of doing business.

A phrase has been created to describe this form of discrimination against blacks, other minorities and women — "the glass ceiling." The glass ceiling describes artificial barriers, based on attitudinal or organizational bias, that prevent qualified individuals from advancing upward in their organization into management level positions. This author describes the glass ceiling as something more hideous than the description above. The glass ceiling consists of invisible, illegal and immoral artificial barriers which impede or prevent equal employment, opportunities, support and salary compensation to African Americans, other minorities and women. While they cannot see or touch it, it is easily felt and extremely painful. Its effects are demoralizing, devastating and often overwhelm its victims. It was created and is supported by unfounded prejudices against minorities and women.

While the glass ceiling may be seen as a step above the former total exclusion of minorities and women from achieving equal opportunities, it still denies these groups full participation in their equal rights. The glass ceiling amounts to an unstable, small and unequal share of opportunities for this segment of our society. The glass ceiling represents broken spirits, unfulfilled dreams, and loss of important contributions to our society. It perpetuates poverty, racial hatred and discrimination, hopelessness, physical and spiritual death to generations of minorities and women.

The glass ceiling provides minorities and women a constant view of what they will never achieve because of their race, nationality or sex. This is a painful and humiliating experience. The glass ceiling creates inequities in hiring practices, compensation, levels of support, and opportunities which are mandatory for successful careers and personal satisfaction. Its activities impede or prevent its victims from progressing into entry, middle, and senior level positions. This ideology is currently supported and practiced by many companies and institutions who publicly state they are equal opportunity employers.

In August of 1991, the findings of the first major study of the glass ceiling by the Labor Department, "A Report on the Glass Ceiling Initiative," was publicly released. The year-long study of the practices of nine Fortune 500 companies demonstrated the glass ceiling exists and is thriving in America's corporations and businesses. This study is the first time the Labor Department or other government agencies have analyzed discriminatory practices and trends of corporations in such a manner to specifically identify biased practices.

Racist and sexist discrimination can no longer be passed off as figments of African Americans' and women's imaginations. It can no longer be viewed as an unimportant issue. In the glass ceiling report, former labor secretary Lynn Martin states,

The glass ceiling, where it exists, hinders not only individuals but society as a whole. It effectively cuts our pool of potential corporate leaders by eliminating over one-half of our population. It deprives our economy of new leaders, new sources of creativity — the 'would be' pioneers of the business world. If our end game is to compete successfully in today's global market, then we have to unleash the full potential of the American work force.

The time has come to tear down, to dismantle the glass ceiling.

The Labor Department made other important and alarming findings during its study:

- The glass ceiling existed at even lower levels than originally estimated.

- Minorities have plateaued at lower levels of the work force than women.

- There is little monitoring by corporations to determine if minorities and women have equal access and opportunities for advancement to lower, middle and senior management positions. This also creates an environment where minorities are not fairly represented in the decision-making process. Corporations have never considered these issues as major concerns or responsibilities. They are not included in fiscal business planning nor as formal policies/procedures.

- Minorities' and women's compensations, reviews and incentives are not monitored for parity, reasonableness or discriminatory practices that limit opportunities and financial rewards.

- Inadequate personnel records are kept. They are needed to properly monitor and determine if affirmative action requirements are fulfilled.

- Employers do not provide affirmative action policies to executive search firms. Positions filled by networking often exclude minorities and women.

- Employers do not extend traditional methods for grooming future management to minorities and women. They do not provide them equal educational assistance, training, coaching. They do not provide them mentors, access to committees, meetings, task forces and other important skills and experience-building vehicles that are mandatory for advancement.

- There is a lack of corporate ownership of equal opportunity ideologies and principles. Senior level executives and policy makers are not involved nor held accountable for affirmative action programs.

The Labor Department study recommended improvements in several areas that would be effective in combating and eliminating the glass ceiling:

1. Extensive educational efforts to educate senior executives to accept the responsibility of diversifying the work force and to be directly involved in the supervision and success of this task. They require that effective public awareness programs encourage companies to improve their methods and procedures of hiring and promoting minorities. Internal education of Labor Department employees on glass ceiling issues is also required to help eradicate these problems.

2. The Labor Department needs to recognize and reward companies that work to develop and implement programs to diversify their work force.

3. Additional studies are required. The Labor Department needs to conduct additional studies and reviews of the working conditions and hiring practices of more Fortune 500 Companies.

4. Encourage aggressive voluntary efforts. The benefits of implementing voluntary efforts to create diversity in the work place must be stressed by showing business and corporate leaders it is in their best interest. Senior members of the Labor Department are involved in this effort. They are participating as speakers, conducting meetings, round table discussions, forums, and are working with the media. Emphasis is placed on the importance of full utilization of the work force to stay competitive and profitable.

Another study commissioned by the Labor Department was to determine the problems employers and employees encountered with our changing work force. This study researched more than 100 companies. They reported their findings, and recommendations in the book entitled, *Opportunity 2000: Creative Affirmative Action Strategies for a Changing Workforce.*

This book made important recommendations which are vital to the elimination of the glass ceiling in our society. In the chapter entitled "Minorities and the Economically Disadvantaged," it identified the inadequate investment in human capital as the most significant problem. It resulted in the failure of minorities to obtain equal status in our work force.

> Because inadequate investment in human capital is the key obstacle today to the full participation of minorities and the economically disadvantage in the workforce, building human capital is the key to efforts by businesses to tap this rich source of labor. And it is the key not only to bringing more minority and disadvantaged workers into the workforce, but to retaining and promoting them" (p.69).

The following is a summary of some recommendations which were made by the study to combat the human capital problem:

- Companies must invest in training employees to ensure they have the abilities to perform their jobs. This also prevents existing skills from becoming obsolete and keeps employees competitive. Minorities and the economically disadvantaged must be included.

- Companies must recognize public schools have failed to adequately train and prepare students for work. Training must be provided to unskilled workers to make them employable. This includes literacy, basic skills and job training. Companies can establish training programs. Working with other companies reduces costs. Partnerships must be formed with public schools. Employers can work with schools to create meaningful courses and assistance. This includes providing managers to teach courses that prepare students for work.

- Companies must establish internships and work-study programs. They are essential to properly prepare young and older employees for the work force. This provides important experience and exposure to employees. Employers receive immediate benefits from the work produced by internship and work-study programs.

- Companies must attempt to recruit and attract minorities and the economically disadvantaged from their communities. This can be accomplished by becoming familiar with minority community resources and learning how to utilize them. Jobs must also be accessible to minorities and the economically disadvantaged. Jobs must be accessible by public transportation and be geographically desirable. Company-sponsored transportation and car pools are vital to the success of these programs when jobs are located outside the inner cities.

- Hiring minorities and the economically disadvantaged is not sufficient to end discrimination and eliminate the glass ceiling. They must make efforts to create and properly manage a culturally diverse work force. This includes establishing career paths for all minority employees. Career paths must be based jointly on employee and company goals, and the available opportunities. Opportunities must be equally accessible to all employees. It is critical that employers design programs to retain minorities and give them equal opportunities for upward mobility.

In August 1992, The Department of Labor released another study, "Pipelines of Progress." It was an update on the "Glass Ceiling Initiative." The report focused on procedures companies can utilize to remove the glass ceiling. It also conducted and or reviewed other significant labor studies. It reviewed a study of 20 Fortune 500 companies by researchers at Loyola University of Chicago and the Kellogg Graduate School of Management. This study reviewed the career progressions of over one thousand male and female managers. The female managers with equal or better education earned on the average less than their male counterparts and held less senior managerial positions. The following are areas of concern identified in this follow up study.

- A lack of consistent recruitment practices to attract a diverse pool of talent. Tracking of minorities' and women's advancement beyond recruitment is generally not performed. Without proper follow-up, progress cannot be monitored or insured.

- A lack of opportunity for minorities and women to contribute and participate in corporate development experiences.

- A general lack of corporate ownership in affirming that the practice of equal employment opportunity is an organizational responsibility, not one person's.

The study found the following procedures were the most effective in combating the glass ceiling:

- Tracking women and minorities with advancement potential

- Ensuring access and visibility

- Ensuring a bias-free workplace

- Entering the pipeline (corporate attention to improve placement of minorities and women into entry-level professional positions).

Another recent study was completed by the "Glass Ceiling Commission," created as part of the Civil Rights Act of 1991. It consisted of a 21-member body appointed by the President and congressional leaders, and chaired by the Secretary of Labor (Robert Reich). The Commission was established to identify glass-ceiling barriers and expand practices and policies to promote employment opportunities for the advancement of minorities and women into positions of responsibility in the private sector. It concluded its study in 1995. A summary of some of the most important findings are as follows:

Eleven Practices of Corporate America that Stifle Advancement of Women and People of Color

1. Initial Placement in relatively dead-end staff jobs
2. Lack of mentoring

3. Lack of management training
4. Lack of opportunities for career development
5. Lack of opportunities for training tailored to the individual
6. Lack of job rotation
7. Little or no access to critical developmental assignments
8. Different standards for performance evaluation
9. Biased rating and testing systems
10. Little or no access to informal networks of communication
11. Harassment and other counterproductive behavior

Summary of the Glass Ceiling Commission's Twelve Recommendations:

1. Eliminating the glass ceiling requires full commitment from CEO, Presidents, and Board of Directors to establish work force diversity policies company wide and actively promote them.

2. Include diversity in all strategic business plans and hold line managers accountable for progress.

3. Use affirmative action as a positive tool to ensure the employment system provides equal opportunity to all.

4. Select, promote and retain qualified individuals.

5. Prepare minorities and women for senior positions.

6. Educate corporate ranks

7. Initiate work/life and family-friendly policies

8. Adopt high performance workplace practices

9. The government must lead by example and increase its efforts to make equal opportunity a reality for minorities and women.

10. Strengthen enforcement of anti-discrimination laws.

11. Improve methods to accurately collect data to determine the progress or lack of progress regarding the advancement of minorities and women.

12. Increase disclosure of diversity data specifically for senior positions.

These studies and recommendations are important steps in publicly acknowledging and confronting minority employment problems. When companies are allowed to conceal discrimination, they will never be forced or inclined to correct the situation. Recognizing and acknowledging discriminatory practices are the first steps required to eliminate this evil from the workplace.

Chapter Eight
THE MYTHS AND THE REALITIES

Until justice is blind to color, until education is unaware of race, until opportunity is unconcerned with the color of men's skins, emancipation will be a proclamation but not a fact.

— *Lyndon B. Johnson*
Speech, Gettysburg, PA, 5/30/63

When we're unemployed, we're called lazy; when the whites are unemployed it's called a depression, which is the psycho-linguistics of racism.

— *Jesse Jackson*
Interview with David Frost, "The Americans," 1970

Many white Americans accuse minorities of unfairly taking their jobs. They perceive minorities as the cause of unemployment and low salaries in the white population. They believe minorities are given preferential treatment at the expense of whites. They believe unqualified minorities are routinely provided employment over qualified white employees to meet quotas. They see this as "reverse discrimination." These perceptions have created resentment and animosity among the white community toward minorities.

Such beliefs are generally based on misconceptions that have nothing to do with the realities of the work place. It is true there have been gains in the work place for minorities and women during the last 25 years. But these gains are mostly limited to entry level and middle management positions. Even given these small advancements, minorities are still subjected to major inequities in the work place. We must learn the facts concerning blacks, minorities, and women. Only the facts can eliminate false misconceptions and prejudices from the work place. As the African proverb says, "Let him speak who has seen with his eyes."

Are Black Applicants Really Given Preferential Treatment?

While whites have blamed all minorities and women at various times for "reverse discrimination," African Americans, and African-American men in particular, are the ones most often singled out. But as we shall see, numerous studies show that affirmative action and other programs have had very little positive impact on black men's employment prospects; ironically, in some cases the manner in which these programs have been implemented have had a negative effect on the African-American community.

A 1991 Urban Institute study showed white applicants were three times more likely to be hired than black applicants. The study involved sending identically qualified black and white applicants to interviews for 476 jobs advertised in Chicago and Washington. The results showed that 15 percent of white applicants were hired compared to 5 percent of equally qualified black applicants. The study also showed that white employees who were hired were promoted 20 percent of the time, compared to 7 percent of black employees, and that white candidates received rude treatment 27 percent of the time compared to 50 percent for black applicants.

The *Wall Street Journal* published an article (September 14, 1993) based on a study they conducted of companies that reported employment data to the Equal Employment Opportunity Commission (EEOC). The article, entitled "Losing Ground, In Latest Recession, Only Blacks Suffered Net Employment Loss," studied job losses of whites, blacks, Hispanics, and Asians for the economic recession of 1990–1991. The study showed disproportionate percentages of blacks were losing jobs compared to other racial groups. While other groups (whites, Asians and Hispanics) showed overall gains in employment, blacks were the only group that showed major losses. This caused a reduction in employment gains that blacks had made in prior years.

The *Wall Street Journal*'s study was extensive. They analyzed changes in employment by race of 35,242 companies from computerized records of 1990 and 1991 EEOC reports. This study included more than 40 million employees, which is approximately one-third of the American work force. The *Wall Street Journal* analyzed increases and decreases in each race category between 1990 and 1991. Next they calculated the percentage change and black job loss index. Based on this information, the *Wall Street Journal*'s study concluded that, overall, blacks lost a disproportionate share of jobs during this period. For example, Bank of America's percentage of black employees in 1990 was 7.9 percent; in 1991, the black percentage of job loss was 28.11 percent, with a black job loss index of 3.56 percent, meaning blacks were 3.56 times more likely to lose their jobs at this company. Another example was Sears, which had a 15.85 percent black work force in 1990. The percentage of black work force reduction in 1991 was 54.32 percent, with a black job loss index of 3.43.

This disparity in the percentage of blacks losing their jobs was the prevailing trend found throughout this study. While companies have stated this was not done intentionally, it has been a factor in the double-digit black unemployment figures. Many civil rights groups believe the black job losses are racially motivated. In any case, studies such as these prove blacks are the ones who suffer the most severe job losses during recessions and difficult economic times. The *Wall Street Journal* study also determined that blacks lose a disproportionate number of jobs involving public-contact occupations. EEOC records showed that blacks lost 5,823 sales jobs during this period. This happened even though companies experienced a net increase of more than 63,000 sales jobs during the same period. White, Asian and Hispanic employees filled these new sales jobs. This substantiates the belief that blacks are the last hired and the first fired.

The Bureau of the Census also provides some interesting facts regarding unemployment among whites and minorities. The civilian work force consists of the non-institutional population 16 years and older. The 1990 civilian labor force consisted of 124.8 million people. The black civilian labor force was 13.9 million, which represents 11 percent of the civilian labor force. By the year 2000 this figure will increase to 12 percent. The national unemployment rate for 1992 was 7.4 percent based on a civilian work force of 127 million. This meant 9.4 million in our labor force were unemployed that year. The unemployment rate for men and women was 7.8 percent and 6.9 percent respectively. The 1992 national unemployment rate for blacks was 14.1 percent. The civilian black labor force 13.9 million. This means 1.96 million (13.9 X 14.1 percent) of the African-American work force was unemployed. This figure represents 20 percent (1.9 million X 9.38 million) of the total unemployed labor force. The unemployment rates for blacks and whites for 1993 was 12.9 percent and 6.0 percent respectively. The unemployment figure for blacks in 1994 and 1995 was 11.5 percent and 10.4 percent, but experts believe the black unemployment rates for 1994 and 1995 were actually higher. The "official" rates exclude the growing numbers of disenfranchised, out-of-work blacks who were not registered for unemployment in the 1994 and 1995 figures. The disproportionate number of blacks incarcerated also reduces the unemployment rate. The decreasing unemployment rates for whites for 1994 and 1995 were 5.3 percent and 4.9 percent.

While African Americans represent 11 percent of the total labor force, they often represent 20 percent or more of the total unemployed population. Since 1974 unemployment rates remained in double digits for blacks. White employees often blame blacks as the reason they are unemployed during recessions. In reality black unemployment reaches its all-time high during recessions. In 1983 national black unemployment rates were as high as 20 percent. In light of these studies and statistics, it is clearly ludicrous to blame African Americans for white unemployment, or to contend that they receive preferential treatment on the job market.

The census also shows that while blacks are still the second-largest minority group, excluding women, in the U.S., the black population increase has been minimal (less than 2 percent) during the last 20 years compared with Hispanic, Asian, and other minority groups. In 1970 the population percentage for blacks was 10.9 percent, Hispanics represented 4.5 percent, Asians and other minority groups represented 1.3 percent. This changed dramatically by 1990; by then, the population percentage for blacks was 12.5 percent, Hispanics 9.5 percent, and Asians and other minority groups 3.8 percent. These figures show that Hispanic, Asians, and other minorities (which include Native Americans and Hawaiians) are the fastest growing segments of our population. Their percentage of the population has doubled in the past 20 years. Furthermore, the percentage of the white population has decreased by approximately 9.1 percent in the past 20 years. In 1970 whites represented 83.3 percent of the population in the U.S. In 1990 whites represented 74.2 percent of the population.

As well as the disparity between whites and minorities, studies such as the *Wall Street Journal*'s and others reveal that all minorities are not receiving equal opportunities for employment. They show a disproportionate number of jobs (in relation to population percentages) are redistributed among certain minorities and non-minorities. This is done at the expense of African Americans, but in the end this does not help any minority group. At any given time any minority group can lose their fair share of jobs if discrimination is unchecked. This becomes a dangerous game of musical chairs. It unfairly compels one group to compete against another for the limited number of jobs available. Getting minorities to fight and discriminate against each other has been an effective tool in the past. It has been used to manipulate and to maintain control over minority groups. Dividing minority interests dilutes the strength minorities find when they work together.

Minorities must be careful not to waste their time or energy fighting against each other. This hurts all minorities and fails to address or eliminate the reasons discrimination exists in the work place. Instead of fighting against each other, minority groups must work together to eliminate all forms of discrimination. This is the only way to ensure each group receives its fair share of jobs. This is the only way minorities can achieve permanent progress and equality in employment opportunities.

Do Affirmative Action Programs Have a Negative Effect on Whites?

Today, 60 percent of the civilian labor force consists of non-white men. Since African Americans only represent 11 percent of the labor force, they do not represent most of the work force. Over the past 30 years, the largest growing segment of the labor force has been women. Many white males incorrectly believe affirmative action programs unfairly denied the white population jobs. They feel they unfairly give jobs to blacks at their expense. Ignorance and prejudice perpetrate this misconception. But if employers do not hire white males because of affirmative action requirements, it is more likely that they hired a white female rather than an African American.

White females have benefitted the most from affirmative action programs. They have received more jobs and benefits than blacks and other minorities. Ironically, while affirmative action programs came about due to black protest, they have helped more white females and other non-black minorities than African Americans. Affirmative action programs were never designed exclusively for blacks, but the public at large believes affirmative action programs mostly benefit blacks. The reason for this common belief is the African Americans' monumental and public civil rights struggle which resulted in affirmative action laws. African Americans are not receiving or retaining their fair share of jobs. This happens because African Americans are often considered the least desirable of minority groups to employers. Deeply embedded prejudicial beliefs about blacks create this perception, which has been in existence for hundreds of years.

This false perception — that unqualified African Americans are using affirmative action and equal opportunity provisions to obtain jobs that rightfully belong to qualified whites — is also an effective tool used by racists to incite whites and others to anger. It helps them recruit others to attack affirmative action and other programs that would promote parity in the work place. To make sure you are clear on who receives benefits from affirmative action, we must review its legal definition. Federal statutes and regulations require affirmative action programs "to remedy discriminatory practices in hiring minority groups: i.e., designed to eliminate existing and continuing discrimination, to remedy lingering effects of past discrimination and to create systems and procedures to prevent future discrimination. . . . Other factors considered are race, color, sex, creed and age."

Affirmative action programs have also been expanded to help the disabled and other disadvantaged groups. Based on federal and state employment figures, very small numbers of white men have lost jobs to blacks because of affirmative action.

Due to economic reasons, women's liberation, new opportunities, and personal fulfillment, more women are entering the labor force. Men can no longer progress in their careers without competing against the opposite sex for jobs at some point. This situation was unheard-of 25 years ago. In 1950 women represented 29 percent of the civilian labor work force; this increased to 37 percent by 1970, reached 45 percent by 1990, and will reach 47 percent by the year 2005.

While women still do not receive a fair share of senior level positions or equal pay, they are no longer restricted to entry-level or "pink collar" positions. Women are no longer denied the professional careers that were once reserved for men. Today, employers are savvy enough to know women can compete on an equal basis with men. Women's abilities are found to be on equal levels with men when they are afforded identical opportunities.

The increase in the number of women in our work force has made it more competitive for men. Regardless of this fact, women have the same rights as men to obtain employment. Denying a woman a job because of her sex is illegal and immoral. With 50 percent of marriages ending in divorce, and the increase in unwed and single mothers, women are often the sole source of financial support for their families. It is no longer a luxury for women to work. It has become a matter of necessity.

The growth of participation by women in our labor force has exceeded marginal gains made by African Americans. The increase in the female labor force has taken more jobs from white males than African Americans ever will. Within the political arena and labor force, our country is changing from a white male-dominated society to one where women will have great influence.

Let us review other facts that show the disparity and discrimination blacks encounter in the work place. These facts clearly demonstrate that African Americans do not receive preferential treatment. The Census Bureau conducted a study in 1989. It showed white college graduates were paid one-third more than black college graduates. Black men with four or more years of college earned on the average $31,380; white men of equal education earned $41,090 during the same period. Black men 25 years or older with four years of high school and with no college education earned on the average $20,280; white men with the same qualifications earn $26,510. Black women in this category earned $16,440 (38 percent less than white males) while white women earned $16,910 (36 percent less).

Recent studies, including *Workforce 2000,* commissioned by the Department of Labor, show that discrimination is having a more devastating effect on black men and Hispanics than any other minority group. In 1987, *Workforce 2000* found that women had 45 percent of jobs, blacks 9.9 percent of jobs (black men 4.8 percent and black women 5.1 percent), while Hispanics had 6.4 percent of jobs. *Workforce 2000* projects these figures will become worse for black men and Hispanics by the year 2000. Women will have 50.5 percent share of new jobs. Blacks' share will be reduced to 9.5 percent of new jobs (decrease of .4 percent). Black men will have 3.8 percent of new jobs (decrease of 1.1 percent) and black women will have 5.6 percent share of new jobs (increase of .5 percent). Hispanics' share of new jobs by the year 2000 will be 5.0 percent (decrease of 1.4 percent).

Do Affirmative Action Programs Have a Negative Effect on African Americans?

In the United States blacks are the only race that has more females employed than males. The Bureau of Labor Statistics stated in 1992, 7 million black women were employed, compared to 6.9 million black men. Studies such as these explain why black men are becoming so susceptible to destruction. Many experts believe they are becoming an endangered species. *Essence,* an African-American women's magazine, produced a special issue entitled, "Race — Black Men Speak" (November 1992). In this special issue *Essence* stated, "African-American men suffer the brunt of America's racist baggage. More than any other single group, black men are the most threatened, so vulnerable to destruction that they are often labeled 'endangered,' and the most threatening, generating fear and suspicion in the hearts, minds and imaginations of most white people."

Often, companies discriminate against hiring black males by intentionally hiring only or mostly black women. This is insidious because it deliberately creates needless confrontations between black men and black women. It is an attack on the black male's manhood and his ability to provide for his family. This has had a disastrous effect on the black race.

The lack of good salaries and meaningful careers creates financial problems in the black family. Financial difficulties are a primary reason for the high rate of divorce. It is a major reason for the large number of single black mothers. Many black women believe black men cannot provide or care for them. Many black females have professional careers and earn more money than their spouses or boyfriends. This has caused black women to lose respect for black men. This is a great source of animosity between black males and females. Many blacks believe this situation has been intentionally created by the white establishment to destroy the image and spirit of black men. This is a factor in the high black male unemployment rate. It has destroyed the ability of black males to succeed in their careers.

There are other reasons why companies hire black women rather than black males. Companies feel less threatened by black female employees. They feel black females will not complain or challenge discriminatory practices. They also believe if black females do complain they are not as adamant as black males. Overall, whites feel more comfortable with black female employees than black males. White employees are inclined to feel more at ease with black females than black males. Another reason is that black females are willing to work for less than black males.

Many whites are unwilling to work with black males and cannot see themselves taking orders from black men. Whites fear black males will become confrontational if they disagree or make them angry, or that black men cannot possibly be qualified to do the work at hand. These are just some reasons why black males are vulnerable to destruction and why they call them an endangered species.

The Census Bureau also showed that the jobs educated African American desire are moving to the suburbs where fewer blacks reside. Data also show educated blacks are more likely to be hired in service-related fields that traditionally pay lower salaries.

Are Affirmative Action Programs Still Needed?

While African Americans have been in the forefront of the civil rights movement for the past 40 years, studies cited in this chapter show blacks have suffered disproportionate losses in employment gains in recent years.

Large segments of the white population complain about laws that favor minority rights. They feel it places them at a disadvantage and believe it is a form of reverse discrimination. We need to examine the reasons why civil rights laws are needed to protect minority rights. The federal government has assumed the responsibility to end discrimination against African Americans since 1866. Most individuals are only familiar with The Civil Rights Act of 1964 and 1991. They are not aware of the other important Civil Rights Acts of 1866, 1870, 1875, and 1968. Acts of Congress passed most of them to specifically protect African American legal rights.

They passed the Civil Rights Acts of 1866 and 1870 to give blacks rights as citizens in legal actions and to ensure they are not denied equal protection because of their race. Prior to this blacks could not bring legal action or own property. The Civil Rights Act of 1875 guaranteed blacks the right to use public accommodations. Ironically, the Supreme Court in 1883 declared it unconstitutional. In 1941, President Roosevelt first encouraged minority employment by ordering defense contractors to end discriminatory hiring practices, but no enforcement or sanctions for non-compliance were put in place. In 1953, President Dwight D. Eisenhower created the first committee to review minority job-discriminatory complaints against federal contractors. This had little impact because they imposed no sanctions against employers who did not adopt or enforce this policy.

Massive black protests and demonstrations during the civil rights movement of 1957 to 1965 led to job discrimination being declared illegal. In 1961, President John F. Kennedy introduced the term "affirmative action." It held government contractors accountable for their hiring practices. Hiring regulations, standards, and sanctions were implemented to enforce these goals. Today affirmative action programs have become misunderstood and offensive to many whites. This includes whites who have benefited from affirmative action through the creation of employment opportunities for them and improvement their standard of living.

Another victory for minorities' and women's rights was the passing of "The Civil Rights Act of 1964." It prohibited discrimination in employment and established the Equal Employment Opportunity Commission (EEOC). This act also banned discrimination in public accommodations connected with interstate commerce, including restaurants, hotels, and theaters. In 1965, President Lyndon B. Johnson issued an order that made it compulsory for all businesses doing business with the U.S. government to have written affirmative action plans. "The Civil Rights Act of 1968" extended "The Civil Rights Act of 1965" to include housing and real estate.

Another important event occurred in 1968. The National Advisory Commission on Civil Disorders concluded that "Our Nation is moving toward two societies, one black, one white, separate and unequal." Unfortunately, this statement is as true today as it was 25 years ago. If you think, this statement is untrue consider the legislation required and passed in 1991.

Congress passed "The Civil Rights Act of 1991" to strengthen federal laws which recent Supreme Court decisions eroded. Congress also recognized they were not achieving the goal of equal employment in the work place for blacks, other minorities and women. The Supreme Court decision, *Wards Cove Packing Co. v. Antonio*, 490 U.S. 642 (1989), which weakened the scope and effectiveness of federal civil rights protection, was a motivating factor in passing "The Civil Rights Act of 1991." Congress also recognized additional legislation was needed due to unlawful discrimination in employment.

The Civil Rights Act of 1991 included provisions to correct deficiencies in the work place as defined in the "Glass Ceiling Initiative." Congress also passed it to provide appropriate remedies for intentional discrimination and unlawful harassment in the work place. They created these civil rights laws and mandates to ensure African Americans, other minorities and women are given equal treatment in employment and in our society. They did not create them to give favorable treatment but to create parity. All benefits from the Civil Rights Act of 1991 were lost due to 1995 and 1997 Supreme Court decisions. As explained in chapter one, the 1995 Supreme Court decision *Adarand Constructors, Inc. v. Pena Secretary of Transportation* severely limited the use of affirmative action to achieve parity in the work place. This decision requires all racial classifications, imposed by whatever federal, state, or local governmental actor, to be analyzed by a reviewing court under strict scrutiny and narrow tailoring.

Even more ominous was the 1996 passage of California's Proposition 209. It is the prohibition against discrimination or preferential treatment by state and other public entities. To quote from the proposition itself, "It prohibits the state, local governments, districts, public universities, colleges and schools and other governmental instrumentalities from discriminating against or giving preferential treatment to any individual or group in public employment, public education, or public contracting on the basis of race, sex, color, or ethnicity or national origin." While this may sound noble, it has in fact reversed the civil rights gains made in the last 30 years. Its passage voided all state and city affirmative action laws and requirements in California.

The small opening that affirmative action made for creating parity in the work place for minorities and women is gone. This law overlooked the illegal discriminatory practices minorities and women endure and the reasons why it was necessary to create affirmative action. Even with affirmative action minorities and women still had fewer opportunities and were paid lower salaries than white males. The purpose of Proposition 209 is to return to the pre–civil rights, white-male status quo. This law had no regard for minorities' and women's rights and the inequalities they endure. This was followed by 1997's Supreme Court refusal to hear arguments against Proposition 209. It was not a surprise that there was not a dissenting vote because the Supreme Court has rejected every race-based affirmative action case brought before them in the last decade.

This is a sad commentary on the highest court in our nation which has engraved above its entrance, "Equal Justice Under the Law," and then refuses to hear arguments on the merits of affirmative action. The Supreme Court's decision gave authority to other states to pass similar laws. A similar measure, modeled after Proposition 209, was recently defeated in Houston, but 21 other states and Congress are considering bills to end affirmative action in public hiring and contracts. White America is staging their own uprisings by enacting laws that are miscarriages of justice against minorities and women.

In less than a year, minority businesses have been devastated by these decisions. A California law that directed billions of dollars to minority- and woman-owned businesses were ruled unconstitutional by the U.S. 9th Circuit

Court of Appeals based on the passage of Proposition 209. This law required that contractors share 23 percent of their jobs with female, minority or disabled veteran contractors. Soon federal government contracts will no longer be required to ensure minorities receive their fair share, and will inevitably revert to the "good old boys" system, which means white males only.

After the Supreme Court's decision, the University of Pittsburgh and other institutions throughout the United States canceled their minority contracting programs. Within this same time period minority enrollment has dropped dramatically in colleges and universities nationwide. In effect this is depleting our country of much needed future minority and women business leaders.

Before the Civil Rights Act of 1964 it was impossible for minorities and women to receive fair treatment. Recent revelations of Texaco executives and their disparaging remarks and attitudes toward blacks prove little has changed in the last 30 years. Racism and sexism are ingrained in our society and have made it impossible for these groups to receive fair treatment. Affirmative action was designed to counteract premeditated unfair treatment created by white America and to promote parity in business, employment and education. We have become complacent with the past gains of the sixties and allowed our greatest victory — affirmative action — to slip away without putting up a fight. African Americans and minorities must take steps to empower themselves before it is too late. We must come together as one. Separately we are weak, but in unity we are a force to be reckoned with.

Is the Government an Equal Opportunity Employer?

Now that we have reviewed an important part of our history, we can better understand and address the difficulties that African Americans, other minorities, and women encounter. Now that we have also reviewed the responsibilities of the federal government, let's study the current facts and progress that our government has made. The federal government is our country's largest employer and has the responsibility for enforcing equal employment laws. Ironically the federal government is also the biggest violator of the laws they are responsible for enforcing. It has done little to enforce affirmative action programs within its own government agencies. In 1989, women held 43 percent of federal positions but were employed in 85 percent of federal clerical positions. The average salary for male employees for this period was $34,430 while female employees' average salary was

$20,015. Minority groups held 28 percent of federal positions but only represented 7.5 percent of senior level positions.

Bernard Ungar, a General Accounting Office analyst, and other government officials have stated that the Equal Employment Opportunity Commission (EEOC) has not vigorously enforced federal employment laws. The EEOC has not been clear on their own policies concerning affirmative action and its enforcement. The EEOC was two years late in completing its plan to eliminate job discrimination in the federal work place; the plan was due in 1988 but was not completed until 1990. Evan Kemp, former Chairperson of the EEOC, stated his department lacked the resources to monitor government agencies or effectively enforce equal employment laws. He blamed Congress for not allocating sufficient funds for his department to properly address these issues or to enforce affirmative action laws in both the public and private sectors.

African Americans, minorities, and women must become politically astute and advocates to control their destiny. Most important, we must exercise our right to vote for candidates that support our interests. We must be willing to participate in protest, boycotts, sit-ins and even go to jail if that what is it takes to insure our rights. We must act now before it is too late.

Are Minorities and Women Moving into Management?

The 1991 report on the "Glass Ceiling Initiative" clearly shows there have been insignificant gains in middle and senior management positions by African Americans, other minorities, and women. The Department of Labor randomly selected, from a pool of 1,000 Fortune companies, 94 corporate headquarters for study. The study reviewed data from more than three years. The population consisted of 147,179 employees. They determined the following facts:

- 15.5 percent of the population were minority employees (22,813).

- 6.0 percent of management were minority employees (1,885 minority employees). The total management population consisted of 31,184 employees. Their positions ranged from supervisors of clerical pools to CEO and Chairperson.

- They employed 2.6 percent of minorities (117 minority employees) in vice president positions or higher (population of 4,491).

- 37.2 percent of employees were women (54,751).

- 16.9 percent were women (5,278) employed in managerial positions. Population consisted of 31,184 employees, their positions ranged from supervisors of clerical pools to CEO and Chairperson.
- 6.6 percent were women (296) employed in vice president positions or higher (population of 4,491).

UCLA Anderson Graduate School and the Korn/Ferry International Executive Search Firm completed another 1990 survey. The survey, "Korn/Ferry International's Executive Profile 1990: A Survey of Corporate Leaders," analyzed data for 10 years (1979–1989). They reviewed the top executive positions of largest 1,000 corporations in our country. The survey found that in 1979, minorities and women held less than 3 percent of the managerial positions. In 1990 less than 5 percent of managerial positions were held by minorities and women. This was less than a 3 percent increase during 10 years.

These are clear indications that minorities and women are not obtaining parity in employment opportunities, financial compensation or receiving preferential treatment in the work place. This phenomenon is not due to lack of abilities, skills, or education in minorities and women employees; these groups are more qualified today than ever before.

These conditions are real. They are the results of artificial barriers imped-ing their progress. They are not unfounded figments of minorities' and women's imaginations. These are real sources of frustration and legitimate reason for concerns and complaints. They are justifications for immediate changes in the treatment toward minorities and women. Change requires more of companies than just advertising they are "Equal Opportunity Employers." They must acknowledge these problems are not myths or invalid complaints. They must understand it is a reality that minorities and women are commonly discriminated against in the work place.

Corporations and institutions are often misled because they believe the small changes made to address this problem are sufficient. They must think again and consider this important point:

"I believe the glass ceiling is real, that it destroys morale, and that though we have made some progress, we are a long way from shattering it."
— *Evan Kemp, Chairperson, EEOC*
"Report on the Glass Ceiling Initiative," 1991

If there were parity in hiring practices there would not be a need or concern for quotas.

Unfounded Beliefs

Blacks and other minorities are frequently labeled as lazy. Laziness has nothing to do with race or color. The perceived laziness of an individual is based on a combination of circumstances. They include one's upbringing, their level of motivation, and their incentives for working. We must also take into account their experiences, beliefs, confidence, skills and abilities. They also commonly label blacks and other minorities as untrustworthy, troublemakers or combative. These qualities have nothing to do with race, color, education or intelligence. Trustworthiness and placidity are qualities which internal values determine. No scientific study deems any race to be more trustworthy or serene than another.

Another fallacy is that African Americans and minorities are not intelligent or good workers. All races have the same capacity to learn and achieve. As in all races there are individuals with different degrees of intelligence and abilities. Too many whites base their relationships with blacks and other minorities on one negative experience. White employers' opinions and actions are often based on unfounded rumors or circumstances that are not the faults of minorities.

One negative incident with a minority should not make you believe all your dealings with them will be similar. They call this stereotyping. White employers and employees frequently stereotype blacks and other minorities. If whites applied this type of logic to themselves, they would be unable to work with white employees or employers again. They should not hold blacks and other minorities accountable to higher standards than whites. If whites can overlook bad experiences with themselves, they must do the same for blacks and other minorities.

Why Don't More Blacks Start Their Own Businesses?

It is widely believed by whites and others that blacks in particular lack the initiative to start businesses. Others believe that African Americans are too dependent on white businesses and need to create black-owned businesses and become self-dependent. This is a valid concern which deserves an honest response and close examination. Based on the recent census information (1990), 7.4 percent of the white population in the U.S. own businesses. The figure is 3.0 percent for blacks. This means 92.6 percent of the white and 97 percent of the black population in the U.S. are employees or unemployed.

Most of us incorrectly believe the white race has the highest number of businesses in relation to the percentage of their population. The ethnic groups with the highest percentage of businesses are Koreans (16.5 percent), Japanese (11.1 percent), Chinese (9.0 percent) and Cubans (8.3 percent). When compared to these ethnic groups, whites have the fifth highest percentage (7.4 percent) of businesses.

Black businesses fall in eleventh place (3.0 percent) of the 13 ethnic groups reviewed. Given the size of the black population, why are there relatively few black-run companies? Black businesses are often more difficult to start because of their lack of access to capital and expertise. This is part of the reason why the percentage of black-owned businesses is so small.

Businesses have traditionally denied blacks access to senior-level executive positions. Becoming a president of a company is almost impossible if you are never allowed to became a vice president or a senior level manager. Denial of senior level positions prevents blacks from being exposed to the inner circle of management. Becoming top sales executives is impossible for blacks if they are never allowed the opportunity to sell million-dollar accounts. This situation has denied blacks the experience, expertise, and confidence to start businesses. Due to this lack of business exposure blacks lack the skills to start successful businesses. Without experience African Americans lack the necessary banking, investment, and marketing skills and savvy to successfully promote their ideas and businesses or expand them on a large scale.

The "Statistical Abstract of the U.S. 1992—The National Data Book," provides valuable insight. For 1987, the number of black-owned firms was 424,165 with annual sales of 20 billion dollars. Hispanics owned 422,373 firms with annual sales of 25 billion dollars. Asian and Pacific Islanders owned 355,331 firms with annual sales of 33 billion dollars. Because of the problems blacks encounter, most of their businesses are small family operations or single proprietorships that operate in their local communities. African Americans' average annual sales are $50,000. Approximately 85 percent of black businesses fall within these categories.

According to more recent Bureau of Census data, black-owned firms' annual revenues have increased to 32.2 billion dollars. This figure represents a 46 percent increase from previous periods. Still, black-owned business only represents 1 percent of total business earnings in the United States. Individual revenue for the average black firm is still less than for other minorities. Average annual earnings of black-owned firms in the U.S. is $52,000 (an annual increase of $2,000) compared to $193,000 for other races. Worse yet, 56 percent of black-owned firms had earnings of less than $10,000. This means they cannot create jobs and provide employment or job training for their communities.

To increase black economic wealth African American entrepreneurs must move beyond mom and pop businesses. Blacks must create industries which provide employment and opportunities. Our business must possess competitive technology and skills. African Americans must create high-tech businesses that create skilled jobs and careers for minorities. Minority business must pay competitive salaries and benefits and provide training to entice the best, brightest and our youth. To accomplish this African Americans must develop the appropriate education, skills and secure suppliers, distributors, lines of credit and viable networks. Black businesses must get involved in our schools and the education of our youth. This is the best way to eliminate unemployment, drugs and crime in our communities.

Generations of African Americans have been denied important skills required to become successful, large-scale entrepreneurs. Without this experience and knowledge they will never learn how to successfully promote black businesses. This prevents African Americans from expanding and competing on regional, national or international levels. Black businessmen, mentors and role models are needed to plant seeds for future black businesses. Successful businesses men and mentors must instill hope in our younger generation. We need successful blacks to share their knowledge and experience. They must not only teach but encourage blacks to establish businesses. We need black business leaders and mentors to teach minorities how to create business plans, raise capital, work with banks and investors. We need them to teach us how to market our goods and services in the most effective ways. Most important, we need them to give us the confidence to succeed.

Blacks must address the problems that confront them. The rules are different for black businesses. Our society has intentionally denied black businesses equal access to valuable resources. These resources include credit, services, vital information, and opportunities. This prevents blacks from successfully competing in the marketplace. Often investors and institutions are unwilling to invest in sound business ideas because the originators are African Americans. This prevents blacks from establishing business and independence for themselves. Often after blacks develop excellent vehicles for success and non-minorities exploit them. Too often black businesses are only able to obtain financing or support if they relinquish control or ownership of their business.

Successful African-American businesses are fighting for survival. Large, white-owned businesses and individuals are taking over traditional black markets that African Americans created. White-owned corporations have created divisions just to capture African-American and other minority markets. This includes white-owned African-American hair and beauty products companies, radio stations, and clothing outlets, just to name a few. Many successful white artists have emulated black styles, music and traditions. They made fortunes while African Americans remain in poverty. This has occurred even before the time of Al Jolson. He was a white performer who sang and danced in a black-painted face. Little Richard and Chuck Berry influenced the Beatles and Elvis Presley. Percy Sledge never won a Grammy for his classic song, "When a Man Loves a Woman," but 30 years later, a version recorded by white heartthrob Michael Bolton did.

Blacks must support black businesses by investing in them to insure their survival and success. Investing in black businesses requires that African Americans develop capital through personal savings, investments and earnings that are available for black entrepreneurs as loans or investment capital. African Americans work to change the negative perceptions of black businesses. This cannot happen overnight but it is an obtainable goal that must be a high priority. The state of black owned business is not promising unless African Americans are willing to move into hi tech industries that create employment, competitive salaries and skills that are in demand. Black businesses must move beyond the confines of local communities and expand to regional and national levels. Once this is accomplished blacks must seek international commerce with Africa, South Africa, Caribbean, Central America, Europe, and Third World countries.

Where Have the Jobs Gone?

Americans are having difficulty finding jobs because of the changing structure of our economy during the last 40 years. Our work place has changed from a manufacturing giant to a service-oriented economy. This has resulted in a huge foreign trade deficit and the loss of millions of manufacturing jobs. In 1950 America imported and exported goods and services totaling nine billion and ten billion dollars respectively. This created a one billion dollar foreign trade surplus. By 1975 our imports were $108 billion and our exports were $99 billion. Our foreign trade surplus increased to nine billion dollars. These trade surpluses created millions of jobs for Americans.

Based on a 1992 report by the National Association of Manufacturers the U.S. experienced two "all time highs" for employment. They related to manufacturing industries during the periods of 1961–1969 and 1975–1979. Manufacturing jobs reached 21 million during these periods. By 1980 this condition had reversed dramatically. America imported 245 billion and exported 221 billion dollars in goods and services. We had a negative 24 billion-dollar trade deficit. This was a negative turnaround of 35 billion dollars within five years. During the 1980–1982 recession manufacturing jobs dropped to 18.4 million. This was a loss of 2.7 million jobs.

In 1985 our trade deficit reached an unbelievable 132 billion dollars. Goods and services trade deficits for 1994, 1995, 1996 and 1997 were 106.2 billion, 111 billion, 111 billion and 114 billion dollars per year respectively. This excess of imports means America is no longer producing the goods it needs. Millions of American manufacturing jobs have been lost to countries such as Canada and Mexico. During 1991 and 1992 manufacturing jobs were still at 18.4 million. At our present rate it appears these jobs are lost forever. In fact it is estimated that an additional 2.2 million manufacturing jobs will be lost by the year 2000.

Our increasing trade deficit results in major losses of American jobs. This has been a major source of unemployment in our country. African Americans, other minorities and women are not the reasons for the loss of American jobs to foreign trade.

Whites believe the reason they cannot obtain jobs is that minorities are taking them. The information I've provided shows minorities have disproportionately low percentages of jobs. The real reasons why many non-minorities are unable to find employment and success in their careers are as follows:

- We now live in a global market that is more competitive. Companies markets' and profits have shrunken. They are forced to eliminate excess costs and waste they once accepted in the past. Companies are downsizing or right sizing to maximize their returns.

- The foreign trade deficit for 1997 was 114 billion dollars. We have become a nation of consumers instead of producers.

- The United States is no longer the manufacturing giant. Companies are not willing to make investments in plant expansions, renovations, and to retrain employees.

- Research and development, and investment tax credits are no longer available to the manufacturing industry. Most American manufacturing companies can no longer compete with the cheap labor in foreign countries. We have failed to develop advanced technology to enable us to compete.

- Legal requirements have caused changes in our work environment. This has resulted in the loss of jobs do to pollution, environment, safety concerns, waste, health cost and benefits, law suits, etc.

- The number of unskilled jobs is shrinking. Most of today's jobs require special skills and training. The less your skills are the more difficult it is to find meaningful employment.

- The duties and demands of jobs are changing on the average of every five years. They must retrain employees in their present positions or train for new ones every five years. This must be done to remain competitive and to stay employed.

- Many professions have become obsolete due to changes in market, new technology and cost inefficiencies. These positions have diminished or they have become extinct.

- Studies have shown that 70 percent of long-term employees are inadequately trained or skilled. They are unable to obtain compatible employment and salaries outside of their current company. If these long term employees leave their present jobs, they will not be competitive in the work place. They will be unable to find employment. They will be forced to take positions for less pay unless they are willing to be retrained. Seven years or more of employment is considered long term.

- Companies are intentionally finding ways to eliminate older workers (legally and illegally). They are intentionally replacing them with younger workers whose salaries and benefits are less costly.

As you can see, none of these reasons has anything to do with minorities taking jobs from whites. They relate to economics, business decisions, legal issues, technology and trends. It is due to a lack of understanding that African Americans and other minorities are blamed for the loss of white jobs in America.

It is discrimination at its worse to deny minorities and women equal opportunities to pursue their careers. They must give each individual the opportunity to compete with others in a non-biased atmosphere. They must allow minorities to progress on the basis of their abilities and efforts. In reality whites should have little fear of minorities unfairly taking their positions. A greater concern should be their level of competence. Instead they should be more concerned with their ability to compete and adapt to the ever changing work environment.

Reverse Discrimination and the Angry White Male

Intense discussions and conflicting views concerning minorities and women receiving preferential treatment are sensitive and highly debated issues. Two common themes that arise in these debates are "reverse discrimination" and "the angry white male syndrome." Reverse discrimination holds that whites are being unfairly discriminated against in employment and other areas (e.g., college acceptance). The angry white male syndrome is the emotional manifestation of white men who believe in reverse discrimination and blame it for all their difficulties in life. Armchair psychologists have used it to explain such things as violent behavior among white men and the growth of white supremacist and paramilitary fringe groups, with the implication that such things are the logical consequence of affirmative action and equal opportunity programs.

The contention of advocates of the reverse discrimination argument is that qualified white males are subjected to employment discrimination. They believe unqualified minorities and women are given jobs that white men equally deserve. Their view is that no group or gender should be subjected to racism or bigotry. This argument has been used effectively to attack and dismantle affirmative action.

A superficial review of the reverse discrimination argument makes it appear to have merit and legitimate claims — discrimination is wrong; applications for jobs or university admission should be based on merit alone.

But in reality, once you understand the basis behind the reverse discrimination argument, you find it is racism and bigotry in its purest form.

The reverse discrimination defense only addresses the symptoms of racism and bigotry that affect a small portion of the white male population. It does nothing to address the roots of racism, bigotry, and sexism that have such devastating effects on the vast majority of African Americans, minorities, and women in our society. It gives no credence to the fact that the white male majority created and supported institutionalized racism, bigotry, and sexism in our country. White males refuse to accept responsibility to eliminate the plague they created in our society.

The reverse discrimination defense is an insult to fair-minded individuals' intelligence. Even the federal government, which is responsible for enforcing affirmative action and overseeing government contracts and is the largest employer of our country, has acknowledged that it has failed to properly disperse contracts and promote and pay minorities and women on an equal scale with white males. The Glass Ceiling Initiative and several follow-up studies of Fortune 500 companies by the Labor Department for the first time verified the existence of an invisible barrier preventing minorities and women from advancing in the working world.

Proclaiming that discrimination and bigotry are sins of the past and white males are no longer responsible is denial. Denial is the infrastructure that sustains and perpetuates racism and bigotry in our culture. The white population must realize that ignoring or tolerating discriminatory activity is the same as supporting it. White Americans who do nothing to eliminate racism and bigotry are as guilty as the individuals who perpetrate these acts. The white male ruling class also overlooks the fact that the necessity for affirmative action came about because they created a demand for it. Contrary to popular belief, minorities and women will praise the day when affirmative action is not needed. Minorities and women cannot accomplish this goal without the support of the white male population.

The white male power structure conveniently ignores the fact that they attached a stigma to professional minorities and woman. White males frequently assumed professional minorities and women obtain jobs because of whom they are and not because of their abilities. They assume minorities are unqualified because of this false stigma. This perpetuates the false belief that minorities receive preferential treatment and do not deserve their jobs.

These attitudes are the reasons why white males disregard minorities' qualifications. This is why they view minorities' expertise, experience, education, and credentials as suspect. This attitude causes them to view minorities' and women's dedication, hard work and accomplishments as trivial. The stigma created by white males makes it difficult for qualified minorities and women to find satisfactory employment. White males should evaluate their prejudices by answering this question: Do you think minorities and women are hired because of whom they are and not because of their abilities? If you do, you possess biased views toward minorities and women.

It is a fact that minorities and women are most often hired because they are the best candidates for the position. Small numbers of minorities may receive preferential treatment, but there are extenuating circumstances to justify these actions. These extenuating circumstances are to eliminate inequities created by past and current discriminatory employment practices. These activities are still rampant in America's work place. The Glass Ceiling Initiative and other labor studies support these facts.

Both the "angry white male syndrome" and the "reverse discrimination" argument are merely updated tactics to mask bigotry and discrimination. This facade creates a marketing image that is attractive to misinformed citizens. It legitimizes these evils by masking their true intentions. This makes reverse discrimination seem plausible and creates sympathy for the angry white male. It is an effective way to ensure the continued existence of racism and bigotry. In recent years much attention and energy has been focussed on dismantling affirmative action. It is an easy target for gutless politicians who want to appear to be taking action, while conveniently distracting the public from the more challenging economic problems that are the real causes of unemployment.

In this chapter I have shown that programs and policies aimed at redressing longstanding inequities in American society have had little negative impact on the employment prospects of white men. Most jobs are lost because of changes in domestic and foreign markets, new technology, environmental issues, obsolescence. Add legal issues, downsizing, global competition, changing job skills, new technical jobs, and elimination of unskilled labor, and you have a complete list. African Americans, other minorities, and women should not bear the blame for white men's failure to succeed.

White males must stop blaming minorities and women for their job losses. Updating or learning new skills, and becoming better informed about economic, political, and social issues would better serve white males, and

> "He that is possessed with a prejudice is possessed with a devil, and one of the worst kinds of devils, for it shuts out the truth and often leads to ruinous error."
> — *Tryon Edwards*

would be more effective than blaming minorities and women for their employment difficulties.

Prejudice and discrimination do not belong in the work place. They only impede everyone's progress and ability to succeed.

Racism and discrimination are wrong. When individuals or a class of people's rights are violated, they have a legal right to seek restitution. In race and gender discrimination affirmative action was the remedy for both blatant and subtle violations of minorities' and women's rights. In reality, affirmative action never opened the door completely; it just cracked it a little.

Chapter Nine
STEPS TOWARD ELIMINATING DISCRIMINATION

Men and nations must use their power with the purpose of making it an instrument of justice and a servant of interest broader than their own.

— *Reinhold Niebuhr*
The Irony of American History, *1952*

Our flag is red, white and blue, but our nation is a rainbow — red, yellow, brown, black, and white — and we're all precious in God's sight. America is not like a blanket — one piece of unbroken cloth, the same color, the same texture, the same size. America is more like a quilt — many patches, many pieces, many colors, many sizes, all woven and held together by a common thread. . . . Even in our fractured state, all of us count and all of us fit somewhere.

— *Jesse Jackson*
Speech, Democratic National Convention, 7/16/84

During the sixties and seventies blacks participated in sit-ins, marches, voter registration drives, and organized strikes. This was done to achieve political power, and to eliminate employment discrimination and other racially motivated practices. Because of this, it is now illegal to discriminate against hiring minorities and women. But, as I have shown, companies involved in these activities now use covert methods to continue this practice. Due to the nature of subtle, covert, and discreet methods of discrimination, new tactics must be used to combat and eliminate them.

When and How Should We Address Discrimination?

The correct answer is a simple one: Address discrimination whenever it occurs. Never use the excuse, "I am waiting for the right opportunity," as justification to ignore discrimination. When we choose to wait, we not only give our permission; we endorse discrimination as an acceptable way of life.

Whenever we address discrimination, we must respond with integrity, intelligence, and honesty. We must use common sense and act with the spirit of God in our hearts. Only by doing this can we successfully eliminate discrimination in the workplace. Silence is discrimination's greatest ally.

"No person is your friend who demands your silence, or denies your right to grow."

— Alice Walker
In Search of Our Mothers' Gardens, *1983*

African-American and Minority Corporate Politics

During the past 30 years, African Americans have held a substantial number of positions in influential political offices. In 1970 there were 48 black mayors. African Americans and other groups accomplished this feat by working together to achieve common goals. As of 1990, African Americans have been elected to head nearly half of the 25 largest cities' political offices. Studies conducted by the Joint Center found in 1993 black mayors represented 356 towns and cities. Former black mayors of major cities include Kenneth Gibson of Newark, Tom Bradley of Los Angles, David Dinkins of New York, Michael R. White of Cleveland, and Andrew Young of Atlanta.

According to the National Conference of Black Mayors this figure has grown to 426 African-American mayors in office in 1998. More than 30 African-American mayors representing cities with populations of 50,000 or more. Large-city African-American mayors holding office in 1998 include Ron Kirk of Dallas (population 1,852,810), Dennis Archer of Detroit (population 1,027,974), Kurt Schmoke of Baltimore (population 736,014), Willie Brown of San Francisco (population 723, 014), Michael R. White of Cleveland (536,000), Wellington E. Webb of Denver (467,610) and Bill Campbell of Atlanta (population 394,017).

African-American legislators formed the Congressional Black Caucus (CBC) in 1971 to obtain better representation in congress. The Congressional Black Caucus is comprised of African-American legislators from the U.S. House of Representatives and U.S. Senate. The CBC acts as a legislative clearinghouse and public information center that addresses concerns of their constituents, national and worldwide issues. They have proved to be a valuable advocate for African Americans, minorities and women.

The 105th Congressional Black Caucus consists of 39 members from the House of Representatives and U.S. Senate. Minorities must understand there is little power when only one individual is willing to address discrimination. When a committed group with common goals addresses discrimination, they can establish a strong power base. This power base can be used to lobby for changes and achieve the goal of ending discrimination in the work place. This is why it is so important to exercise your right to vote and support individuals, parties and companies willing to create parity in the work place.

Progressive corporations support and work with minority organizations. The Xerox Corporation has a national African-American organization within its company. Many Xerox locations have local chapters such as "Los Angeles African-American Engineers & Professionals" and "Los Angeles African-American Employees." TRW also has a multiracial organization called TRW-Space Park Employee Association—Bootstrap (TRW-SEA Bootstrap). IBM also has several organizations to help minorities. One organization is "Motivating Our Students Through Experience" (MOSTE). It is a mentor program through which professional minorities work with minority students to improve their education.

If your corporation does not have one, work with other minority employees to establish similar professional organizations. Contact companies or one of the organizations previously discussed. Ask them for assistance or information on how to start a similar organization. Prior to starting one you must define the specific purposes of your organization. It must be established for positive and legitimate reasons. The purpose of your organization should be in writing (by-laws). The following is an example:

> The Coalition of African-American Health Care Employees was established to promote a positive atmosphere for African-American employees. Its goal is to ensure fair and equal treatment in promotional opportunities and working conditions. We also created this organization to enhance personal development and continued education for minorities within and outside the corporate environment. Our goals are to establish positive rapport with minority employees and the corporations they serve. We accomplish this by working together to promote racial

harmony based on moral and ethical work standards and principles. We desire to resolve all racial related problems fairly. We also pledge to assist in the development of social and economic programs. The primary goal is to educate and assist the poor and disadvantaged.

Any work-related minority organization must mutually benefit minority employees and their employers. If properly organized, such an organization can be a powerful resource. You and your co-workers, and ideally your employer, can use it to eliminate discriminatory practices where you work.

Economic Boycotts

We must identify corporations and companies that engage in racial discrimination. The next step is to orchestrate public campaigns to apply pressure on them. Enlist community groups and organizations to help you. Utilize churches, political or social arenas, government agencies and watchdog groups. Find organizations in your area that are willing to help.

Newspapers, TV and radio stations are interested in these stories. They report them on local and national levels. News organizations have investigative reporters. They can conduct independent investigations which can be beneficial. Politicians and others who hold political offices will sometimes help in these matters. Utilize your mayor, Congress person, city council members and state Senators to help you.

Another possibility is to organize well-planned boycotts of these corporations' goods and services. African Americans, for example, spend 400 billion dollars annually on consumer goods and services. Many companies would no longer be profitable if African Americans boycotted their goods and services. This is a powerful and effective tool that would quickly get American businesses' attention.

Publicized boycotts and protests can be devastating to a company. A company's image is their most important asset. Companies and corporations spend billions of dollars annually to protect and promote their images. One adverse event can create negative publicity. This can tarnish a business's image forever. This adverse image results in lost revenues from not just the minority population. They will adversely affect other segments of their market. These strategies and pressures will result in reduced profits or losses for businesses. Without profits, businesses cannot exist. These tactics are effective in forcing companies to have second thoughts about allowing discrimination to continue.

Sometimes businesses quickly respond and act toward eliminating discrimination within their organizations. In other cases it may take a considerable amount of time. These types of public pressures must be maintained until corporations and companies show they are willing to make the necessary changes.

Dialogue on Racism and Sexism

In 1904, Dr. W.E.B. Dubois, founder of the of the NAACP, said that "the problem of the twentieth century would be the problem of the color line." Almost a hundred years later racism and sexism are two of the greatest problems that America faces. They have the potential to destroy this great country, yet we treat them as if they were cultural taboos. They continue to exist because America refuses to properly address them. Instead of coming to terms with these issues, America treats them as if they were dark family secrets not open for discussion. They are subjects that too many Americans avoid at all cost. We must ask ourselves why racism and sexism are so difficult to discuss. Too many of us avoid this topic because we have guilty consciousness. We dislike our own views but are unwilling to confront them or make changes in our behavior. When we are forced to discuss these issues we are forced to confront our personal shame. This makes us uncomfortable and defensive.

Open and honest dialogue must start from within. We must be honest with ourselves. When we lie to ourselves it is impossible to be truthful with others. We must examine our motives, points of views and beliefs. Are we comfortable with them? Do we need to change our points of views? Do we have the courage to face our fears and to change the things that are wrong with us? Only by asking these questions can we freely discuss the issues at hand and be willing to take the necessary actions to correct the things that are wrong.

President Bill Clinton has recognized the issue of racism will not go away unless we are willing to discuss our feelings and work out our differences. He showed great courage on July 14, 1997, when he announced his intention to launch a year-long dialogue on race in America. President Bill Clinton appointed a seven-person advisory board with the mandate to lead that national discussion. A compulsory part of the dialogue will be that "America must confront and deal with the attitudes and beliefs that one individual or individuals are inferior to another. Attitudes that make one American discriminate against another American because of race or ethnicity."

The Congressional Black Caucus supports President Bill Clinton's actions and stated, "Because of America's volatile history involving race, we believe that it is critical to the future of our country to foster an honest and straightforward dialogue among the races. This is especially true between blacks and whites." All Americans must become willing participants of this dialogue that openly and honestly addresses the problems of not only race but sexism as well. We must include friends, neighbors, coworkers and family members. We must share and respect others' views and create viable solutions to resolve our differences. We must not limit our views to our personal perspective but include the experiences of others as we develop our opinions. Americans must commit themselves to eliminating the scourge of racism and sexism. It is the only cure for the affliction of discrimination.

Chapter Ten
ACCEPTING OUR RESPONSIBILITIES

We must realize that our future lies chiefly in our own hands. We know that neither institution nor friends can make a race stand unless it has strength in its own foundation; that races like individuals must stand or fall by their own merit; that to fully succeed they must practice the virtues of self-reliance, self-respect, industry, perseverance, and economy.

— *Paul Robeson, Actor, Singer, Activist*
Famous Black Quotations

Chance has never yet satisfied the hope of a suffering people. Action, self-reliance and the vision of self and the future have been the only means by which the oppressed have seen and realized the light of their own freedom.

— *Marcus Garvey*
Philosophy and Opinions of Marcus Garvey, *1923*

While these two powerful and motivating thoughts provide inspiration, and hope to minorities and women, they do not reflect the particular indignities blacks experience in America. More than any other minority group, blacks are currently in a state of chaos and crisis in America. Johneta B. Cole explained it this way: "Crisis seems to be too mild a word to describe conditions in countless African-American communities. It is beyond crisis when in the richest nation in the world, African-Americans in Harlem live shorter lives than the people of Bangladesh, one of the poorest nations of the world" (Speech, NAACP Convention, Los Angeles, 7/9/90).

This deplorable condition must be a wake-up call for African Americans in this country. Blacks must change attitudes, beliefs, and perceptions. They must focus their efforts in a new direction. They cannot wait for the white population and their institutions to help them, treat them fairly or eliminate discrimination. African American must develop self-reliance and self-suffi-ciency. It is a waste of time and energy to sit back and complain about unfair conditions and neglect to take action.

Minorities and women cannot afford to wait and hope for laws or the moral consciousness of America to eliminate employment discrimination and poverty. Many Civil Rights Laws have been passed since 1868 and as recently as 1991. Yet poverty and discrimination continue to exist and grow at an alarming rate for blacks, other minorities and women. The sad truth is even when laws are passed to protect the rights of minorities, they are often too expensive and difficult to enforce.

> **"It is difficult to pull yourself up by your boot straps when you don't have any boots."**
> **— Martin Luther King**

Impoverished minorities cannot afford to wait for free handouts or government subsidies to sustain themselves. Minorities and women must learn to depend on themselves. This must not be done just for minorities' success but for their survival. This is not an easy task. Daniel Deleon explained this problem in these terms: "Poverty breeds lack of self-reliance" (*Two Pages from Roman History,* 1903).

Minorities and women must heed the words of Frederick Douglass, former slave, black abolitionist, orator and author: "We must not only be able to buy black boots, we must be able to make them" (*Life and Times of Frederick Douglass).* Blacks and minorities must learn to make their own boots. This must be done if they want to pull themselves out of poverty and eliminate employment discrimination. Minorities and women must accept responsibility for their successes and failures. It is each minority's responsibility to work productively to eliminate poverty, racism, and discrimination wherever and whenever they encounter it.

The only way African American and other minorities can become self-sufficient is to discard negative mental and emotional baggage they carry. Minorities must conquer their doubts, fears, excuses, shame, bad habits, and their mistrust of other minorities. Minorities must throw away phrases such as "I can't do it," "it is too difficult," "it will take too long," and "they will not let me do it." Minorities must see their "burdens" as their source of "power." They must use negative situations as the motivating force that ignites them, use this negative force to break down the barriers in their lives. Adversity builds character when we use it to improve our lives.

African Americans must not only provide for their individual needs and those of their families; they must provide for their race. To create success for themselves, blacks must be willing to do more than help friends and family.

They must be willing to extend helping hands to other minorities in need. To accomplish this blacks must establish important short- and long-term goals that guide them to success.

First, more African Americans must make the transition from black employees to black entrepreneurs. Blacks must develop much more than small mom and pop businesses. They need to create businesses that employ more than family members. Black and other minorities must create small, medium, and large businesses and corporations. They must provide small-, medium-, and large-scale employment opportunities for blacks and other minorities. This is the one way blacks and other minorities can eliminate poverty, employment discrimination and unequal justice in our society.

"When we are noted for Enterprise, Industry, and Success, we shall no longer have any trouble in the matter of civil and political rights."
— *Frederick Douglass*
Life and Times of Frederick Douglass

While there is an urgent need for medium and large black-owned businesses, the importance of small business must not be overlooked. Based on studies by the Small Business Administration, small businesses create the largest number of new jobs. Small businesses are defined as those with 20 employees or less. In 1976, companies with 20 employees or less created 21 percent of new jobs. During this period 48 percent of new jobs were created by large companies which employed 500 or more. By 1982, small companies created 39 percent of new jobs while large companies created 38 percent of new jobs. This trend has continued. Today small businesses create two out of three new jobs.

The way to eliminate double-digit black unemployment and poverty is clear. Blacks must make the transition from being black employees to becoming black employers. Blacks must also stop being just consumers. They must become the diverse producers of quality goods and services.

This is the only way to create employment, financial security, and opportunities for blacks and other minorities. Black creating jobs and opportunities for the black community are the only way to reduce black on black crime, violence and drugs in our communities. Blacks creating challenging employment opportunities that provide competitive salaries and training is essential to the success of the black race.

It will be a major factor in reducing the disproportionate percentage of incarcerated African Americans. Addressing the inequities in the legal system is another factor that needs to be corrected. While African American represent only 13 percent of the population, they represent 45.3 percent of our state and federal prison population. The lack of job and educational opportunities are important reasons for this dilemma. These conditions are also the stimuli for the increase in gangs and violence in our society.

African Americans must be willing to create businesses that create attractive, high-paying and rewarding professional careers for blacks. Good jobs provide employees and youths hope for their future. Only by blacks creating professional and financially rewarding careers can we eliminate black poverty and raise our standard of living. Quality professional careers allow blacks to afford excellent medical treatment they have been denied in the past. It is important to stress that careers are much more than jobs. The emphasis must be on creating professional, rewarding careers, not just jobs. Jobs are something we do to earn money to survive; a career is something we do for fulfillment and in the process earn a respectable living. For ease of reading the terms career and jobs are used interchangeably in this book.

When blacks create jobs in their communities, they create an environment of safety. This is the only way blacks and others will invest in and rebuild their decaying communities. Blacks must develop the skills to create manufacturing jobs, technical jobs, hi-tech jobs, white and blue collar jobs for their communities. Minorities cannot limit their business and employment opportunities to a single industry. Even more important, African Americans must keep abreast with the latest trends and technological developments.

This will only be possible when African Americans and other minorities trust and respect each other as human beings. Only when this happens will minorities be able to successfully work together. There has been limited success in creating employment opportunities because blacks and other minorities have been unwilling to work together. They have failed to come together to create small, medium and large businesses that create independence. They have been unwilling to pool their resources to create jobs, provide training, and share valuable experience. This has caused minorities to lose valuable opportunities for themselves and others.

Once businesses are created, it is vital that black consumers' dollars are recycled back in their neighborhoods and businesses. According to Jawanza Kunjufu's book, *Black Economics,* African Americans' disposable annual income is estimated at 400 billion dollars. The following are other important facts from his book:

- Their $400-billion disposable income ranks the African-American community as the ninth wealthiest nation/colony in the world.

- Only seven percent ($21 billion) of the $400 billion is spent within African-American businesses and communities. This means 279 billion black dollars are spent outside our communities. This creates jobs and wealth for non-blacks.

- Every billion dollars spent outside the black community is equivalent to exporting 10,000 black jobs to non-blacks. Based on this calculation, if African Americans recycled their 279 billion dollars back into their communities, it could create an additional 2.8 million jobs for blacks.

Koreans, Japanese, and Chinese communities are successful in America. It is because they recycle 90 percent or more of their income and wealth back into their communities and families. These ethnic groups also pool resources to promote the growth of their communities and race. They create cooperatives so that small businesses can purchase goods and products at discounts. They create lending institutions that specialize in providing loans to small and new businesses. These ethnic groups place great emphasis on owning businesses, property, savings and investing in the future.

They effectively use the family unit to create wealth. They aggressively promote family businesses and work as a unit to achieve success. They also create collateral and investment capital through personal savings. This is something African Americans have traditionally failed to do. In fact American personal savings are less than other industrialized nations. White Americans save 4.8 of their annual incomes as compared to less than 2 percent for African Americans. West Germans save 14.4 percent of annual income, the French 15.5 percent and Japanese savings are 20 percent. Personnel savings, self sufficiency, property, and investments are the key ingredients to creating wealth.

Unfortunately, African Americans have been unwilling to work as a unit. They are conditioned to seek security in a pay check. Blacks are discouraged from starting businesses by white institutions, other blacks and well-meaning family members. This is unfortunate because being employed by others rarely creates wealth. Blacks have also been conditioned not to trust other blacks and minorities. In many cases, blacks and other minorities work against each other because of trivial matters. They allow petty feelings, personal likes or dislikes, to prevent them from working together. White society intentionally created many of these situations. For blacks, most of these problems stem from attitudes ingrained in our culture since slavery.

One of the most effective tools slave owners used to control slaves was the technique of dividing and conquering. Slave owners created and ingrained mistrust, hatred, and jealousy within the slave population. These lies and negative stereotypical images are still common today. Slave owners effectively made the black slave population dependent on their owners for survival. To ensure their dominance and control, slave owners made it illegal for slaves to receive any education, learn to read or write, and own property. Whites treated blacks differently based on the lightness or darkness of their skin — the lighter the skin the better the slave was treated. This indoctrinated blacks to discriminate against themselves because of the different shades of their color. The few blacks given power over other black slaves were required to keep them under strict control.

These blacks were expected to be more brutal to other slaves than the white slave owners themselves. They had to do this to keep their position and receive special privileges. Blacks have carried many of these negative attitudes into the twentieth century. Today instead of blacks being physically chained and caged, they are kept imprisoned within their minds. Over the last four centuries blacks have been conditioned to think in this manner. This is far more dangerous than being a physical slave.

Blacks must be the first ones to stop perpetuating black stereotypical images, negative beliefs, and prejudices within their own communities. Blacks must work to disprove these inaccuracies. They must show a willingness to support other blacks in their business endeavors. Blacks must support black businesses that provide quality goods, services and jobs for their communities. Blacks must learn to network, support and invest in each other. Only when blacks accomplish this will other minorities and races fully accept and respect the black community as equal business partners .

African Americans can become their own worst enemy. This happens when they allow others to manipulate them into discriminating against themselves. This not only limits blacks' chances for success, it destroys them.

Minorities must be willing to put aside petty differences and work to resolve misunderstandings. African Americans and other minorities must realize the importance of working together for the common good of their people.

Because of poverty, unemployment, and the lack of respect, blacks develop negative attitudes. They start to believe the stereotypical images about their race. African Americans have been divided into two main groups: those who have very little, and those who have nothing. The ones who have nothing are trying to acquire from the ones who have very little. The ones who have very little are struggling to keep what they have from the ones who have nothing. This struggle perpetuates anger, jealousy, a lack of unity, and disrespect among African Americans. This is why African Americans commonly say, "I won't do business with other African Americans. I don't trust them," "I don't like their service," or "they charge too much." It is unfortunate adults teach this negative thinking to their children and anybody who will listen.

This type of thinking becomes embedded in our minds and we start to believe this type of negative and untruthful thinking. It becomes a vicious cycle that just continues to repeat itself. This type of negative attitude and thinking even carries over into our personal and professional lives. This thinking creates environments where African Americans are unwilling to support each even when it is in their best interest.

African Americans must first start with themselves. They must work to eradicate negative beliefs or circumstances they encounter. Before you subscribe to the myth that all African-American businesses provide inferior goods or services, do this. Take the time to remember past incidents. You can probably recall when you received poor goods or services or were overcharged by non-black-owned companies. Now take the time to recall when you received excellent goods and services from African American businesses. The truth is, we receive good and bad services from all nationalities, races and genders.

Next, African Americans must come together in harmony with other minority groups. This starts by taking the time to respect and understand the diversity of other cultures. Minorities must look past the lack of trust, cultural differences, stereotypes, rumors, and negative experiences. Negative attitudes, stereotypes and unfortunate circumstances caused minorities to lose sight of important facts. It is important minorities work together to improve working conditions. It is a waste of time and energy focusing on what we do not like about each other and other non-minorities.

Minorities and women must not emphasize negative incidents or myths about themselves. Instead they must focus on and promote their achievements. Minorities and women must be willing to become role models and set positive examples for others. Minorities must be willing to tear down counter-productive and useless barriers. We must be willing to extend the hand of fellowship to all minorities and women without exception.

African Americans must develop dialogue and communicate to bridge the gap between our younger and older generations. Dialogue must be of a positive and productive nature. Blacks and other minorities must be willing to give of themselves. This must be done without asking or expecting anything in return. Blacks must not only give advice but accept advice when it is in their best interest.

Too many African Americans do not know how to read and write. They only need someone to volunteer a small portion of their time. They desperately need someone to show a little interest and a willingness to teach them. Blacks must learn the importance of sharing their knowledge and skills with other African Americans. Blacks and other minorities must learn this valuable lesson: When we help others, we help ourselves. We not only become better human beings in the process but we create bonds. These bonds create life-long customers, support for our ideas, products and services.

Most African Americans have no sense of history nor pride about themselves. They desperately need someone to teach them about their glorious past and the current achievements by African Americans. This knowledge develops self-worth and fellowship within our communities. African Americans and other minorities must realize success is not about individual accomplishments. Instead they must learn that each individual is a small part of the big picture. Each individual has a responsibility. It is to share, teach and help others to become a success. Only by doing this can each individual become a true success.

Minorities accept responsibility for their success when they establish and commit themselves to worthwhile goals. Regardless of your goals, they are lacking if you fail to include learning and understanding God's word. God's teachings show they require that you work to rid our society of discrimination, racism, and sexism. It is each minority's and non minority's responsibility to commit themselves to achieving this goal. Minorities must willingly commit themselves to achieving parity in all facets of employment. Equality means receiving equal opportunities, support, authority and financial rewards. They must never look upon this responsibility as a burden. It is an opportunity to improve your life, and your family and our society. Always remember, "We Cannot Grow If We Are Never Challenged."

Assimilation Is Not the Answer

While minorities and women must commit themselves to creating equality in our society, we must realize it will never be accomplished without achieving financial independence. African Americans have made the mistake of placing too much emphasis on assimilating into white America. This is not a call for segregation. It is a call to become self-sufficient. In the late sixties as soon as limited opportunities became available, African Americans who reaped the benefits abandoned the inner cities and the people who needed them the most. Middle class and affluent blacks fled to the suburbs and robbed inter cities of resources required for their survival.

Without black financial resources, role models and business inner cities have moved into a new level of despair. In too many black communities, the major industry is crime. Too many blacks believe the only means of earning a living it to sell drugs. This is not the only option available. African Americans who have achieved success must be drawn back into the black communities to help revitalize them. African Americans cannot wait for white America to fix this problem.

Blacks must develop black businesses in their communities that not only create meaningful employment but careers, new businesses and entrepreneurs as well. Inner city residents must be willing to pool their resources to create an environment conducive to attracting new businesses. Poor, middle-class, and affluent blacks must all work together to create a climate that promotes independence for their people. Affluent and middle-class blacks must understand that without the support of the poor black population they cannot maintain their wealth and success. Without them they do not have a foundation that will support them when the tides change.

African Americans are not the only group who has spent too much effort trying to assimilate. White females have also expended too much effort trying to be part of the white male boys club. This attitude will only ensure that a selected few white females will succeed. These chosen women are sometimes forced to become something other than a woman to obtain and maintain their positions. Many of these women become so caught up in the male mentality they feel threatened by other women and are unwilling to help other females succeed. Instead of women concentrating on being one of the boys, they must develop networks and support groups that help more women create businesses, careers and independence. Women must be willing to support and encourage other women to succeed. The female gender must realize they should not to give up their rights to be a woman to succeed. Women must never believe that they are of less value than men. Succeeding is about what you can do. It has noting to do with your gender.

Other segments of minority groups have also abandoned their race to assimilate into the white culture. They have denounced their kind, changed their names and religions to blend in with white Americans. All races lose when this occurs. We lose our values, important parts of our history and valuable resources needed for our communities. More important, when we fail to love and respect who we are we lose the most important part of ourselves. No race or gender is better than another. We all succeed when we respect ourselves and others who are different. We must heed the words of author Alex Haley:

> In all of us there is a hunger, marrow-deep, to know our heritage, to know who we are and where we have come from. Without this enriching knowledge, there is a hollow yearning. No matter what our attainments in life, there is still a vacuum, and emptiness and the most disquieting loneliness.

Chapter Eleven
CHANGING THE CORPORATE CULTURE

Where after all, do universal human rights begin? In small places, close to home — so close and so small that they cannot be seen on any maps of the world. Yet they are the world of the individual person; the neighborhood he lies in; the school or college he attends; the factory, farm or office where he works. Such are the places where every man, woman and child seeks equal justice, equal opportunity, equal dignity without discrimination. Unless these rights have meaning there, they have little meaning anywhere. Without concerned citizen action to uphold them close to home, we shall look in vain for progress in the larger world.

— Eleanor Roosevelt
Speech, "The Great Question," United Nations, 1958

We can no longer tolerate the old, outmoded values and longtime discriminatory practices levied at minority employees. Efforts to end discrimination must be vigorously carried out by senior management. They must enforce it all the way down to entry-level positions. Chief executives should go on record publicly stating racism and bigotry no longer will be tolerated within the ranks.

This cannot be a once-a-year speech; it must be a daily commitment. It must be given more than lip service. Companies must strive to become a community of one. As the Reverend Martin Luther King warned, "We must learn to live together as brothers or perish apart as fools." Thus, management must be willing to take strong actions against employees who advocate or practice discrimination. They must hold all employees to this standard, regardless of position. There should be no exceptions to this rule. The disciplinary action should be as severe as the infringement. They should terminate employees for extreme infractions. They must make company leaders aware that discrimination is a serious crime. They can eliminate it from the work place only if policy-makers commit to change. They must be willing to enforce new, more equitable standards.

Employees and companies will be persuaded to change only when there are compelling reasons. The most compelling reason is "it is in our best interest." To encourage business to change we must show them the short- and long-term benefits they reap if they modify their behavior. When benefits are real and obtainable they create incentives for companies to change. Related benefits are increased productivity and profits, higher employee morale, reduced employee turnover, elimination of needless litigation, and a safer work environment. Employers will discover a new sense of full employee participation working collectively to ensure the longevity and success of the company.

Another effective method to eliminate biased attitudes is to develop meaningful classes and seminars. They must create honest dialogue and solutions for "real life" discriminatory and racial problems. To be effective, classes and training seminars must encourage participants to openly discuss problems without fear of retaliation. Several important topics that they must cover are:

- Understanding the Benefits of Diversity
- How to Communicate with Different Cultures
- Sensitive Training for Different Ethnic Groups
- Eliminating Negative Beliefs about Others
- How to Successfully Incorporate Different Cultures into a Corporate Life Style.
- Foreign Languages
- Business Ethics
- How to Avoid and Resolve Conflict

> **"Prejudice is being down on something you're not up on."**
> **— Anonymous**

These are just a few of the important topics that must be addressed to successfully develop solutions for eradicating cultural barriers. Other issues depend on the needs of business. They must be adopted into the corporate lifestyle and receive senior management's support. These classes and information sessions are beneficial for creating respect and understanding among different ethnic and racial groups.

People do not realize their views are biased. Prejudiced views allow individuals to see only what they want to see. It makes them oblivious to the truth.

Classes and seminars that promote understanding and provide reliable information are important. They teach different races to see situations from other cultures' point of views. We often justify our improper actions by finding ways to justify our discriminatory practices.

"A great many people think they are thinking when they are merely rearranging their prejudices."

— *William James, psychologist and philosopher*

It is vital, for the successful elimination of bigotry, that we learn and understand different cultures. By learning about each other's cultures, histories and views we eliminate differences between individuals. We find we have more in common then we have differences. We also discover that our goals are very similar.

Educating white employees even when they believe they are not prejudiced is important. Many whites believe they are not prejudiced. They feel they treat blacks fairly, but harbor conflicting views. One belief is strongly anti-discrimination while the other belief is racist in its purest form. This is a paradoxical view that whites often have about blacks. Raymond Mack, a white sociologist from Northwestern University, sees these two conflicting beliefs that whites have about blacks as "that all people are created equal and that blacks are inferior" (Mark Whitaker, "White and Black Lies," *Newsweek*, 9/15/93, p. 54). These conflicting views create a dilemma. Minorities become victims of a white society even when the discrimination is not intentional.

When blacks show they are not inferior and become successful, the white society does not see them as normal blacks. This is why whites fail to give recognition to the black race for the important contributions made by black businesspeople and employees: they see the successful ones as exceptions to the rule. They do not look upon them as normal black successful employees. This dilemma places black employees in a no-win situation.

To eliminate discrimination these myths and beliefs must be destroyed. Only education and replacing inaccuracies with the truth can accomplish this. Educating all employees, from the highest to the lowest, is the only way to change corporate culture. Once we begin to change the corporate culture it is easier to develop policies and procedures that are fair and equitable to all employees. This happens when all employees are allowed equal access to success and opportunities. Instead of viewing the differences in people,

"Brotherhood is the very price and condition of man's survival."
— Carlos P. Romulo

employers and employees learn to see others as partners for success.

Once they develop this partnership, they equally motivate all employees to share in the rewards based on their contributions. Each employee now has a personal stake and becomes a partner in the success of the company. Changing corporate culture requires creating an atmosphere of equal opportunity.

Why Corporations Fail

This book has discussed the importance of changing conditions for minority and women employees in lower and middle management. They must be given equal opportunities to reach their full potential. There is another major change in corporate philosophy that must be made. This philosophy has a profound impact in creating success for American businesses. It will also be a catalyst for the success of minority and non minority employees. Large percentages of businesses never achieve nor retain long-term success because they fail to possess the ingredients for success.

They call this ingredient "leadership." Most business leaders (e.g., presidents, managers, and supervisors) are not true leaders. They are poor imitations of true leaders. They are pseudo leaders. Their shortcomings are felt throughout the organizations. This results in the failure or poor performance of companies and the misuse of their employees. Companies can neither grow nor prosper without true leaders. As we explore the qualifications of leadership, we will learn how they relate to racism and discrimination.

Poor leaders fail because they lack essential qualities for leadership. They fail to understand the purpose of leadership. True leaders know leadership has nothing to do with race, size, appearance, or education. True leaders know their primary responsibility is to serve others. Service must always be for worthwhile purposes as defined by God. True leaders never abuse their leadership privileges for selfish gains. Leaders are not true leaders if greed, fame, power, and pride motivate them. Hatred, discrimination or revenge cannot guide them. They are not worthwhile purposes and not agreeable to God's will. They will always result in their downfall.

The second responsibility of a leader is to produce, cultivate, encourage and promote leadership within all employees. This ensures the continuity of leadership. When business leaders fail to promote leadership for all employees, they violate a key principle of successful leaders. Any individual who is placed in a position of leadership and fails to enforce this principle never becomes an effective leader. This happens when so-called leaders deny African Americans, other minorities, and women opportunities to become leaders within their organizations.

Business leaders fail as leaders when they fail to identify and train potential leaders. This promotes an atmosphere of stagnation and resentment. Company leaders fail as leaders when they create an atmosphere where they operate as bullies. Their main purpose is to control, limit, and restrict the growth of segments of the work force. This not only stunts the growth of employees but that of the company as well.

Leaders who conduct themselves in this manner lack a worthwhile purpose. They lack integrity, morals, and courage. They display selfishness and ignorance of the true meaning of leadership. These pseudo leaders generally create environments of fear to control and manipulate their subordinates. They never allow others the freedom to express their ideas, feelings, and concerns without fear of retaliation. These leaders allow their authority and power to corrupt them. Once this happens they destroy the principles of leadership. They conduct themselves as if they are above the review of their subordinates and others, including God. This is always a fatal mistake.

Let's review the real-life actions of a company president (a pseudo leader) in a senior level meeting who failed to function as a true leader. This president failed to motivate and provide opportunities to employees to grow as leaders and to make valuable contributions. During a meeting, this corporate leader asked each of his subordinates to give their opinions on recommendations made during a meeting. Each subordinate disagreed on the recommendations made by the presenter. After his staff disagreed, the president loudly pronounced that he felt the recommendations were great. He then gave a menacing look to each of his subordinates as if they had done something wrong. The president never bothered explaining the reasons why he disagreed. Immediately each of his subordinates looked at each other. One by one they changed their opinions and agreed with the president.

By the expression and actions of the president's subordinates, I know they were in fear and would never disagree with him. This incident reminded me of the children's fairy tale, "The Emperor's New Clothes," by Hans Christian Andersen. In this story two swindlers conned an Emperor who was obsessed with new clothes. The two swindlers posed as weavers who could weave magical clothes that were the most beautiful in the world. They told everyone their clothes had magical qualities. People could only see them if they were worthy of the office they held. To anyone who was unfit or a fool the magical clothes appeared invisible. The Emperor, his courtiers, and the townspeople were unwilling to admit they could not see the new clothes being weaved.

The Emperor and others allowed fear and false pride to control them. Because of this they failed to show good judgement and admit they could not see the clothes being woven. When the weavers said they had finished the clothes, the Emperor held a parade to show off his new clothes. The Emperor paraded naked through the streets, listening to the crowd yell out how beautiful the clothes were. The people in the crowd were also too ashamed to admit they could not see the clothes. Suddenly a child glanced upon the Emperor and screamed, "The Emperor has no clothes!" Until someone gave the Emperor an honest answer and admitted the truth, he did not realize how stupid and wrong he had been.

This fairy tale illustrates how important it is for true leaders to promote honesty and openness when he or she consults with others. A leader's council must not be placed in a position of fear where they can speak neither the truth nor voice opinions. When this happens, their opinions and support become useless and have no real value. While leaders are responsible for final decisions, they should never make decisions without all the important facts. It is their council's responsibility to provide the facts, regardless if the information is good or bad. Information must be as accurate as possible. Reliable information is critical in making wise decisions.

A leader will never receive all the important facts if he or she creates an atmosphere where their council fears to speak truthfully and openly. A leader cannot be a true leader if he cannot accept other points of view and valid criticism.

"Criticism is the leader's greatest test of maturity, conviction and commitment to his vision. If you are ready for criticisms, you're ready for leadership."
— *Myles Munroe,* Becoming a Leader, *p. 158*

To be successful in leadership, leaders must be challenged by others to bring out their full potential. Henry Ford explained it this way: "My best friend is the one who brings out the best in me." This happens when you are presented with worthwhile challenges and work intelligently to overcome obstacles.

During the same meeting described above, the president showed other poor qualities indicating lack of true leadership. The president looked at his watch and said that he would have to leave immediately because his wife was cooking dinner. He said he had to be home by six o'clock or his wife would be upset with him. One of the president's subordinates stated that the presentation would be over shortly. The subordinate also explained the president's calendar was booked solid for the next month. If the president left, it would delay important decisions for a month. The subordinate tactfully asked the president to stay a little longer so he be able to make his final decisions.

The president looked at his subordinate and said his wife would be upset if he were late for dinner. He then said that if his wife was upset he would be upset. Then he would be upset with them. He then asked, "You do not want me to be upset with you, do you?" The subordinates immediately replied no. The president left for dinner.

True leaders must accept the responsibility to lead and teach. They must provide for the well-being of their families. They must never take family problems or other personal frustrations out on their subordinates. They must accept the consequences of their own mistakes and problems. You see, this president had set up two appointments which conflicted with each other. He was unjustly going to make others suffer for his mistakes. True leaders accept full responsibility for their mistakes and decisions. They do not blame others for their mistakes and actions. True leaders never make others suffer or become the victims of their frustrations or personal problems.

Leaders who show the poor leadership qualities this leader displayed will always be kept in the dark about important information and issues. This information is critical to their success, the success of others and the success of their company. These types of irresponsible leaders will be the first to blame others for not informing them of important matters. In reality they make themselves unapproachable and are not open to others. They keep themselves isolated. They do not deal with problems they feel are unimportant. These same problems are often important to their companies and employees. These leaders only show concern when these problems threaten their own positions. This attitude leads to their downfall and to the company's failure.

A true leader will not use the excuses "I did not know" or "they never informed me of the problem." When leaders do not know what is going on in their company, they have failed as leaders. It shows they created an environment of repression, fear, ignorance, and poor communications, and lack interest in the welfare of others and their company. This only confirms they are pseudo leaders and are unfit to lead.

Perfect examples of pseudo leaders are corporate leaders who say they are unaware of obvious discrimination problems in their organizations. This is especially true when companies publicly state they are "Equal Opportunity Employers" and have affirmative action programs in place. Something of this magnitude is a major responsibility of leadership and the company. It is an important measuring stick to determine the effectiveness or ineffectiveness of leaders. It determines their leadership role and the company's commitment to equal opportunity.

If a company and its leadership are truly committed to the goal of being equal opportunity employers, it must be a function that they closely monitor. They must consistently evaluate it to determine if they are achieving their objectives. This task must not be monitored casually. Subordinates who do not have the authority or interest to correct related problems should never be the ones named to monitor it. If management only becomes aware of the problem when minorities and women complain about discrimination, it shows that they have failed to properly lead others and achieve their objectives.

Now, let's return our focus to the qualities of true leaders. True leaders promote the success and growth of all employees in their companies. Myles Munroe in his book, *Becoming a Leader,* described leadership as follows: "Leadership consists basically of two components. The first is vision and values; the second is inspiring and motivating others to work together with a common purpose" (p. 31). When leaders allow companies or employees to discriminate against minorities and women, they do not motivate or inspire all employees to work with a common purpose. In fact they create dissension and conflicting purposes for different segments of their employees. Luke chapter 11:17 states, "Every kingdom divided against itself is brought to desolation; and a house divided against a house falleth." True leaders understand this and work to promote harmony within the ranks of their employees.

True leaders know the proper way to lead others is by understanding this simple concept: "The purest form of leadership is influence through inspiration . . . Inspiration is the opposite of intimidation and is absent of manipulation" (Myles Munroe, *Becoming a Leader,* p. 32).

True leaders view everyone as a potential leader. They understand it is their responsibility to bring out this leadership potential within all their employees. Real leaders understand the number of new leaders they create determines their true measurement of success. The more leaders a company develops, the greater opportunities they have for success.

For corporations and companies to be successful they must be wise in choosing their leaders. They must pay attention to leadership values and qualities. They must pay less attention to race, sex, friendship and outward appearances. They must select leaders with moral strength and conviction who have a true desire to serve others. They must be committed to worthwhile spiritual purposes. They must provide equal opportunities for all employees to achieve and share in the success of their efforts. They must be willing to allow all employees equal opportunities to become leaders. They must create the desire to participate in common goals which are in the best interest of all parties.

Companies must become color and sex blind in their search for leaders. They must look for leadership traits and qualities in their future leaders. They must select leaders who show independence, self control, trustworthiness and reliability. They must have the ability to inspire others, be approachable and be willing to accept others as they are. They must be peace makers and individuals who have the abilities to accept and learn from constructive criticism. When companies educate and elevate themselves to this level they will find continued success and profits. It will be a natural and permanent part of their businesses.

Chapter Twelve

THE EDUCATION OF CORPORATE AMERICA

A competitive world has two possibilities for you. You can lose. Or, if you want to win, you can change.

— Lester C. Thurow
Interview, "60 Minutes," CBS, 2/7/88

I never varied from the managerial rule that the worst possible thing we could do was to lie dead in the water of any problem. Solve it. Solve it quickly, solve it right or wrong. If you solved it wrong, it would come back and slap you in the face and then you could solve it right. Lying dead in the water and doing nothing is a comfortable alternative because it is without risk, but it is an absolutely fatal way to manage a business.

— Thomas J. Watson, Jr., former president of IBM
Fortune, *1977*

Small business owners will tell you their very survival depends on their ability to recognize and reward merit. With the changing demographics of the workforce, we must make certain that the recognition and reward of merit are both gender and color blind in every sector of our economy.

— Lynn Martin, Secretary of Labor
Press release, 8/11/92

American businesses must educate themselves in their dealings with minorities. Companies must realize employees are their most important resources. Success-oriented companies would consider it foolish and poor business practice to misuse or destroy their assets, investments or resources. No successful companies vandalize their equipment, burn their money, or raze their buildings. If it were determined management was destroying company assets, squandering major investments or resources they would be fired. Management must take the same approach with its minority employees.

When minorities are mistreated and discriminated against, this creates an atmosphere of resentment and discontentment. Instead of an atmosphere where there is a positive and conducive working environment, it is a place of anger, frustration, resentment and limitations. This type of environment is not conducive to performing to the best of one's ability. Napoleon Bonaparte explained it best when he said, "Ability is of little account without opportunity."

When proper fuel or energy is not provided for equipment, it no longer functions. It is the same with human resources that are not nurtured. They cannot operate properly or yield a good return. Eventually they will cease to function and become a liability. This is not fault of the equipment or resources but of the individuals who are responsible for their care. American businesses must realize minority employees are major investments and resources in this diverse and global market. Minority employees can make major contributions to companies only when they are properly treated. If they are not, they can become major liabilities.

To be successful, businesses must learn new ideas to eliminate discrimination and bigotry from the workplace. They must realize the old way of doing business is not working. It is a major liability. Companies must be willing to develop new schools of thought to manage a culturally diverse work force. This idea is explained in *Opportunity 2000*: "Acculturation is not simply a matter of assimilation of individuals into the corporate environment; it is a matter of corporate evolution as well."

Companies must be willing to address discriminatory problems in a way that is productive to the company and its employees. They must not make minority employees feel alienated in their work environment. They must treat minority employees as partners who will share in the success or failure equal to their contributions. Corporations must eliminate past biased customs and unwritten laws used to impede the success of and alienate minority employees. These unhealthy working conditions have devastating effects on minority employees' and corporate performance.

> A climate of alienation has a profound effect on black personality, particularly on the educated black, who has the opportunity to see how the rest of the world regards him and his people. It often happens that the black intellectual thus loses confidence in his own potential and that of his race. Often the

effect is so crushing that some blacks, having evidence to the contrary, still find it hard to accept the fact we really were the first to civilize the world.

— *Cheikh Anta Diop, historian*

To ensure the success of businesses and their employees, new environments are required to ensure unrestricted access to prosperity. Initially there may be some difficulties in finding this balance, but it is worth the time and effort once it is achieved. Changing corporate attitudes can accomplish this: "Companies must view each and every employee as a candidate for advancement." (*Opportunity 2000*) This requires establishing meaningful career paths for every employee. They must be based on employees' and company's goals and be equally accessible to all employees.

Artificial barriers (i.e., unnecessary job requirements, isolation, and intimidation) must be eliminated to allow unrestricted opportunities for success. Dismantling artificial barriers includes eliminating excuses for not developing diversity programs to hire and maintain long-term successful minority employee relationships. They are no longer valid. One such excuse is that the economy is so bad businesses cannot afford to recruit minorities and women. This excuse is invalid as explained in an article in the *Nation's Business* magazine, "Winning With Diversity" (September 1992).

> "People say it's just an awful time, and I say this is the time to plan," says Ann Morrison. "This is the time to structure the kinds of things you can do now and the kinds of things that you will do." Then you'll be ready when the growth starts and there are more jobs, promotion opportunities, and money, she says. "If it is not planned now; it won't happen later."

The article also provides the following eight ideas to help a company create and manage a diverse workplace.

1. Determine the company's needs (identify diversity problems, present and future).

2. Learn all you can (learn the facts that relate to diversity).

3. Curb your assumptions (overcome stereotypical views regarding minorities).

4. Build diversity into your leadership team (incorporate minorities into all levels of management).

5. Expect backlashes and take steps to minimize them (develop plans to overcome diversity problems).

6. Make improvements in communication a company goal (communications must be open, honest and sincere).

7. Expect problems between groups of employees (tough choices and compromises must be made).

8. Look for ways to adjust your company to your workers. (The needs of employees must be incorporated into the goals of the company.)

Companies, minorities, non-minorities and women must understand: No one should be hired nor promoted solely on the basis of being a "minority" or "non-minority" or due to their sex. There must be other criteria to consider. By the same token, no minority nor non-minority should be denied employment, promotions, financial parity, or opportunities because of their race or sex. If companies and employers followed this simple idea there would be no need for quotas or affirmative action programs. When companies fail to honor their legal and moral obligations they should be penalized. Actions must be taken against companies and individuals who practice discrimination. Punishment should include financial reimbursement, rectification of the situation, disciplinary action, and monitored compliance.

Corporate America should correct this situation without the need for outside action or intervention. Companies must accept the challenge. They must have the courage to discipline employees who are guilty of these infractions. The only way this approach will be effective is when offending employees are punished appropriately, regardless of their position or connections in the company. Businesses must exist for more than the creation of profits and personal gain. They also exist to create jobs, opportunities, and growth for the company and its employees. They must exist for the well-being of their customers, by producing quality goods and services for the society which they serve.

Making Prudent Investments in Minority Employees

All viable companies must invest in the future, whether it is technology, equipment, or research. Corporations must realize it is in their best interest to invest in their minority employees. Developing minority managerial training and internship programs create a valuable source of future managers. This is prudent business for companies. It prepares them for the future. It's also important to train existing managers to work fairly with minority employees. Companies should develop workshops to review common discriminatory complaints. This information can then be used to develop workable solutions to eliminate these problems and prevent them from occurring in the future.

Internal review boards should be established to review discriminatory complaints. They should consist of non minorities and minorities. They should review all complaints based on the facts and not the individuals. Resolving all complaints will not be easy. With the proper effort from all parties, workable solutions can be found. American businesses must learn that it is in their best interest and a matter of their survival to make changes that ensure their future success. Companies incorrectly believe they become losers if they give up power or control to their employees. They believe the more they give up, the more they lose.

Nothing could be further from the truth. When businesses empower their employees, they make them accountable. It gives them the resources and incentives to make major contributions to their organizations. Employees become part of a committed team when management learns to recognize and utilize the valuable knowledge they possess.

Management must understand they strengthen their financial position by treating minority employees fairly. One of the greatest challenges of the future will be the ability of management to give up some of their powers. For their employees, the challenge will be to accept this important responsibility and use it wisely. Companies must learn they are the winners when they treat all employees fairly. Businesses may forfeit minimal short-term gains, but are rewarded by the long-term gains of the future that guarantee their success. This only comes about when employers are willing to make responsible changes that are fair and in all parties' interest.

A perfect example of this is when Henry Ford startled the world in 1914. He voluntarily raised his employees' wages. Corporations and businesses thought Ford was crazy when he decided to pay his employees $5.00 a day. This was unheard of then. The business community and others believed the salary increases would reduce the company's profits and quickly put Ford out of business. This did not happen. By doing this, Henry Ford created a new class of workers who could afford to purchase his Model T Ford.

Henry Ford's actions increased his company's sales and profits. This also allowed workers to purchase other goods and services which stimulated our nation's economy. After this other employers also raised their employees salaries to equitable pay scales. Henry Ford made another bold and innovative change: He voluntarily reduced his employees' work week by a day. People again thought Ford was mad and believed it would ruin his business. But Ford's decision gave his employees and other Americans more leisure time. Family weekend drives and outings became a national pastime. This created an even greater demand for Ford's cars and again increased his company's profits, as well as his employees' morale and performance.

Corporations and businesses must take the time to learn from these valuable lessons. In the end it is often beneficial to voluntarily change or make concessions. Companies often learn the changes they make or what they lose is the source of their past failures. Others would have been the source of their future demise if they did not change. Companies should always consider these important lessons when dealing with African Americans, other minorities and women issues. With the ongoing population changes, minority groups will represent close to 50 percent of the population in our country in the near future. With the opening of global markets, different nationalities and countries will be vital components of most businesses' success. They will not only be vital employees and important partners, but also the consumers who will buy their goods and services.

The U.S. Department of Labor's "1995 Consumer Expenditure Survey" esimated that African Americans' and Hispanics' annual consumer expenditures are more than 500 billion dollars (available after taxes and savings). These amounts will increase dramatically in the near future. Successful corporations of the future will be those which create bonds with minority groups to attract them as equal employees, partners, and consumers. They cannot be successful if they use their minority employees as tokens or figure heads. They will need the expertise of these employees to help create and define new markets, create goods and services, and to service their customers at all levels.

American and foreign corporations are creating successful partnerships. They are providing important benefits and advantages that could not be achieved without their combined resources. Successful companies will develop the tools and expertise to work with minority employees. They will view them as important partners and not just employees. This starts by first learning how to successfully work with minority employees. This will only happen when employers stop seeing minority employees as inferior and responsible for taking white jobs. Instead they must see minorities as important contributors, equal partners, important consumers, and as new markets which create new jobs and growth for everyone.

Chapter Thirteen
THE SUCCESS FORMULA

Minorities must develop successful traits and attributes to achieve success. To be successful, grow to the point where one completely forgets himself; that is to lose himself in a great cause.

— Booker T. Washington
Up from Slavery

There are two ways of making money — one at the expense of others, the other by service to others. The first method does not "make" money, does not create anything; it only "gets" money — and does not always succeed in that.
— Henry Ford
Success Forum, October 1928

Winning the gold is important but if you are not enough without it, you will never be enough with it.
— John Candy's coach character in the movie Cool Runnings

African Americans and other minorities must understand success does not happen by accident, luck, or chance. Success is not achieved based on one's race or level of intelligence. Being a dedicated and committed worker does not make you successful. Even being a caring and deserving person does not make you successful. If you take the time to study successful people, you will find most of them have similar qualities and traits. Many studies have confirmed these qualities exist in successful people. It is these qualities and traits that make them successful, and not the individuals themselves.

First, successful people never allow real or imaginary obstacles or disabilities to prevent them from achieving their dreams and goals. They do not allow their race, lack of education, fears, or other so-called obstacles prevent them from succeeding. They learn to believe in themselves and their abilities to achieve their goals.

Secondly, they have a clear idea of what they want long before they achieve it. They design their lives in a way that will help them achieve their mission in life. Na'im Akbar, explained this concept in his book, *Visions for Black Men*. He stated, "Human Progress requires a Vision." The sooner an individual defines his or her vision, the sooner he or she will achieve success. Successful people take the time to develop well thought-out written plans to achieve their vision. They use them as guides to achieve their goals. Their written plans include dates and time frames to motivate them and monitor their progress.

Successful people never sit back and admire their written plans or dreams. They are willing to take constant and consistent actions to achieve their missions. They are willing to take these actions regardless if they receive financial reward, are paid unfairly or receive no pay. They understand they can use their experience, contacts, and knowledge to help them achieve their ultimate mission.

Successful people learn valuable lessons from their mistakes. They do not ignore nor hide mistakes. Instead they see mistakes as valuable experiences which draw them closer to success. Successful people have the inner strength to quickly admit their mistakes and correct them. They do this without carrying a sense of guilt that often paralyzes unsuccessful people for the rest of their lives. They learn effective ways to view and minimize their mistakes. They see and understand mistakes for what they are. Mistakes must be viewed as valuable experiences to enhance your life. Do not make the same mistake twice. When you repeat the mistakes, it shows you learned nothing from your experience.

Minorities and women cannot be successful if they fail to prepare themselves to respond and overcome discrimination. It is inevitable that minorities will encounter discrimination and must develop special skills to succeed in spite of this condition. As Floyd and Jacqueline Dickens describe it in the preface to their book, *The Black Manager,*

> Corporations and other institutions represent a microcosm of our larger society. Racism pervades every walk of our lives, and presents barriers to success for the minority person in addition to whatever his or her individual shortcomings may be. For that reason, the minority managers must acquire additional coping behaviors other than those acquired by managers in general.

Another attribute of successful people is that they are not satisfied with their current and past accomplishments. They do not rely on how things were done in the past. They have strong desires to learn and improve themselves. They constantly seek new ways and answers to improve themselves and their situations. They are willing to develop new ways and methods to improve their performance and chances for success. Successful people do not change things just for the sake of change. They make changes to improve the quality of their own and others' lives. Successful people are willing to take reasonable risks to achieve success. They determine if risks are reasonable by answering these four questions:

- What is the worst thing that could happen?

- What is the best thing that could happen?

- What probably will happen?

- Can I afford not to take the risk?

Minorities must understand they do not have to be the "first" to be successful. Being first does not guarantee success. It does help. But being versatile and able to adapt quickly to important changes in your environment is more important. Successful people are able to recognize opportunities and take advantage of them. They have the keen ability to see potential obstacles as opportunities for success while others see them as barriers.

Important Tips

Find a mentor. Most African Americans in the corporate world never had mentors to teach them the secrets of success. Seek individuals who are successful and who share your ideas and goals. Use them as mentors. There is nothing wrong with asking someone you respect for advice. Identify which skills, traits and knowledge they possess that make them successful. Incorporate these qualities into your lifestyle.

If you do not have the opportunity to obtain a mentor at work or in your personal life, find them in books. You can learn their secrets as you read about them. There are excellent books to read that will provide you with valuable information and inspiration. One of my favorite books is *Think and Grow Rich: A Black Choice* by Dennis Kimbro and Napoleon Hill.

Develop business networks to advance and promote yourself. Develop power bases within and outside your corporation. These business contacts can open doors for you and others within and outside your organization. Learn to self-promote yourself successfully within your organization. Many talented individuals' accomplishments and achievements go unnoticed because they never receive recognition for their efforts or work.

Stay on top of new trends and developments in your field of expertise. Always look for new methods and procedures to improve your performance. Master them and incorporate them into your life. Learn how to create and maintain a positive image. Project your "personal power" when you meet individuals. Show confidence, poise, knowledge and personality. First impressions are the most important. They are based on your appearance, ability to build rapport and speaking skills. Dress in a manner appropriate for your environment.

> "Be skilled in speech so that you will succeed. The tongue of a man is his sword and effective speech is stronger than all fighting."
> — *The Husia*

Hone your public speaking skills. The art of public speaking is critical to success. The ability to speak confidently in public, whether it is to an individual, a president, or group, develops inner confidence. You must learn to be persuasive when speaking. The ability to win people over is the difference between success and failure.

Develop written skills to properly express your ideas. They must be sufficient to create interest and to persuade others to support you. Often we must communicate with individuals or the public by using written or electronic documents. They form opinions and impressions about the writer based on how well they express themselves.

Identify leaders within and outside your organization. Find people who have talents for leadership. Seek people who can raise the consciousness of people. Study them and emulate their skills, presence and abilities. Utilize their talents. It only takes one person to make a change. Remember Reverend Martin Luther King, Mahatma Gandhi, and Rosa Parks. These are just a few of the people who effected change in our society.

Minorities must take the time to learn and master the art of human relationships. Learn to develop meaningful and rewarding professional relationships instead of creating enemies and obstacles to your career.

Never allow negative experiences or people to pollute your mind with hatred or violent thoughts. Taking revenge will only result in your downfall. Remember: We can do the right things for the wrong reasons. This dishonors your achievements. Whenever your heart is filled with pain or evil thoughts and before you make rash decisions, repeat this verse to yourself: "Do not be overcome by evil, but overcome evil with good" (Romans chapter 12:21).

Martin Luther King explained it this way: "We must combine the toughness of the serpent and the softness of the dove, a tough mind and a tender heart" (*Strength to Love,* 1963). If you can create the strength and conviction within yourself to follow this important advice you will find happiness and success in your life.

> **"When dealing with people, remember you are not dealing with creatures of logic, but with creatures of emotions, creatures bristling with prejudice, and motivated by pride and vanity."**
> **—Dale Carnegie**

To be successful in your career you must have a passion for and strong belief in what you do. Having passion and believing in what you do are the driving forces that propel success. Your passion and belief will sustain you in times of adversity. They will provide you with the courage and strength to overcome any obstacles you encounter. Take this advice from Ray Charles: "I don't sing a song unless I feel it. The song don't tug at my heart, I pass on it. I have to believe in what I'm doing."

Real success is based on truth. Never run from the truth; learn how to embrace it. Make it work for you.

"Truth is proper and beautiful in all times and in all places."
— *Frederick Douglass*

Know the difference between fact and fiction. Overcome and move past negative stereotypes associated with race and gender. They represent excess baggage which prevents your success. Learn to see limitations and weaknesses as opportunities for improvement.

A common belief of blacks is that they must be twice as good as their white counterparts just to achieve the same levels of success. This is a source of resentment and anxiety for the black race. Whites will not acknowledge this fact. They believe this is just an unfounded excuse for the failure of blacks. The best expression of this point is:

"He who starts behind in the great race of life must remain behind or run faster than the man in front."

— *Benjamin E. Mays, educator*

Blacks and other minorities should realize there is nothing wrong with being twice as good as others. The problems exist when you do not use your talents and skills to enhance your life. Unfortunately, this is the dilemma for many minorities and women. They have been conditioned them to work for others and not for themselves. If your employer does not take advantage of your skills and talents, they are the losers. Use your skills and ability to start a business. Become the master of your destiny. Minorities and women can only lose when they fail to utilize their abilities in the best possible manner. It is each individual's responsibility to use their skills and talents to enhance their lives. Accept responsibility for your success. Use your talents to create happiness and financial freedom for yourself. Never turn this power, control and responsibility over to your employer. If you do, you will never succeed or find happiness.

This will not be easy. It will be an ongoing struggle throughout our lives. See this personal struggle for what it is. It is the burden we must bear to achieve success. Once we understand this concept, it will make our burdens bearable.

"If there is no struggle, there is no progress. Those who profess to favor freedom, and yet deprecate agitation, are men who want crops without plowing up the ground. They want rain without thunder and lighting. They want the ocean without the awful roar of its many waters. This struggle may be a moral one; or it may be a physical one; or it may be both moral and physical; but it must be a struggle. Power concedes noting without a demand"

—*Frederick Douglass*

I would like to leave you with one final thought on success:

"Your success is not determined by what you have but by what you do with what you have"

— *Myles Munroe*

This statement gives everyone the power to be successful in life.

Chapter Fourteen
LEGAL ALTERNATIVES

It may be true that the law cannot make a man love me, but it can keep him from lynching me and I think that's pretty important.
— *Martin Luther King, Jr.*
Wall Street Journal, *11/13/62*

What we succeeded in doing in the sixties was in dealing with the constitutional issue of rights. We've won that battle . . . [Now] we're dealing with real equality.

— *James Farmer*
American Chronicle, *1987*

Federal and State laws guarantee minorities and women specific legal rights that protect them from discrimination. Unfortunately, it is not easy to prove that these rights have been violated. It is costly and time consuming to prove a case in court. The winner in a job discrimination case is often determined by who has the most money and best attorneys. This is generally the employer. It has nothing to do with who is right and who is wrong.

For minorities and women to improve their chances of winning, they must properly document acts of discrimination, harassment, retaliation, or wrongful terminations. The more your evidence meets the legal definitions the greater your chances of winning. It is possible to win. Many minorities have won legal discriminatory suits against their employers. Generally, attorneys take on employment discrimination cases when clients can pay large fees up front, unless you have a high-profile case. Let's face it. Most individuals cannot afford to pay an attorney to handle their cases. This is stated not to discourage minorities and women. It is simply the truth. It would be misleading and unfair not to forewarn of this situation.

Pursuing legal actions can be costly, time consuming, and frustrating. My answer to this is anything that is worthwhile is not easy. The greater the challenges the greater the rewards. The rewards are a lot more than monetary gains. Become a person of whom you are proud. You will receive the personal satisfaction that you have helped to make this world a better place.

Legal action should only be taken as a last resort and only for valid and worthwhile reasons. Make sure you have exhausted all alternatives prior to seeking legal action against your employer. Your decision to take legal action must not be based on emotions or revenge. It should be based on protecting your legal rights and to improve future conditions for you, your family and other minorities. It is important to understand when one minority protects their rights they are also protecting the rights of others.

Prior to taking legal action, make sure you are knowledgeable of your rights and the laws that protect you. To accomplish this, take a trip to your local law library. Ask the librarian to show you where the laws are pertaining to employment discrimination. You can also speak with a qualified and honest attorney specializing in employment discrimination cases. They can advise you of your rights. Often the initial consultation is free. If they charge a fee, find out in advance how much it is. Just like anything else, be prepared to shop around for a good attorney.

Exceptional attorneys are honest and willing to spend quality time with their clients. They actively listen to what their clients have to say about their case. After they have the facts, they explain appropriate laws to their clients. They also explain the pros and cons of your case and their options in layman's terms. Make it your responsibility to learn and understand state and federal statutes pertaining to your legal rights. Understanding your rights can mean the difference between success and failure in any actions you take.

Discrimination, harassment, retaliation and wrongful termination are the four areas in which civil rights employment lawsuits tend to be pursued. In layman's terms and for our purposes, these are defined as follows:

1. Discrimination — Being treated differently (unfavorably) than others. This happens if you were not hired, denied promotion, demoted, paid unequal wages or unfairly fired, because of your race, color, age, religion or sex.

2. Harassment — to irritate, torment persistently, to wear out or exhaust an individual because of their race, color, age or religion. These actions can be in the form of:

- Verbal

- Pictorial, visual or written

- Physical

3. Retaliation — Inappropriate conduct by employers in response to an employee complaining about situations such as discrimination. By law employees have the right to complain about racial discrimination or harassment within or outside of a company. It is illegal for a company to retaliate against employees for doing this.

4. Wrongful Termination — When individuals are terminated from their jobs due to injurious, needless, unjust, reckless, unfair infringements of their rights. If they fire an individual because of their race, age or sex it is a violation of their civil rights and is a wrongful termination.

Generally, cases of racial discrimination, racial harassment, retaliation and wrongful termination are difficult to prove. Most cases are proven by circumstantial evidence, which consists of:

- Total Work Environment

- Incidents of Discrimination

- Inferences of Discrimination

If your intent is to pursue legal remedies you must show proof of incidents or situations that fall within the four definitions defined. If you cannot do this, you do not have a valid case. If you have legitimate grievances that fall within one or more of these definitions (discrimination, harassment, retaliation or wrongful termination) you have a case for legal action.

Be prepared, whether you use an attorney or not. Your information must be factual. Never fabricate stories or incidents. Be able to show you are a real victim. Be able to explain and prove your charges in terms of the legal definitions. Do the following to ensure you have the proper information and facts to substantiate your case:

- Think! Focus only on the issues and facts — they must be objective and not based on your emotions. Think of your case in terms of the four legal definitions required by law to justify your charges.

- Review your notes. Get the facts clear in your mind. Put them in chronological order by year.

- Review your documents. Make sure you fully understand them and that they support your case. Put this information in chronological order by year. If you are still employed, review your personnel file. Request copies of all pertinent documents. If your employer will not provide copies, take notes of specific information that is appropriate to your case.

- Once you complete your review process, briefly summarize all of your pertinent facts. Type them neatly and record them in chronological order by category (racial discrimination, racial harassment, retaliation, and wrongful termination).

- Show you have a case by presenting pertinent facts. Your information, documents and proof must be provided in a way that a layman will understand. This is critical during court proceedings. This means it must be understandable by others who are not in your profession. It must be presented clearly. Anyone with just a high school education must be able to understand it quickly and easily.

Never make idle threats to your employer. Don't tell them you will take legal action when you know you will not. You will only lose credibility and it will eventually backfire. If you do decide to take legal action, if possible, do it with a group of other employees who are also experiencing discrimination problems. This is known as a class action suit. A class action discrimination suit makes your case stronger by showing there is a pattern of discrimination. This may also reduce your legal fees. All parties involved share the cost. This also puts more pressure on the corporation you are suing. It may result in a quicker disposition of your suit.

Make sure you select an attorney who can properly represent you. Employment discrimination cases require an attorney who is an expert in this field. Make sure the attorney you retain has adequate experience in this type of legal action. Ask questions. Learn the percentage of cases they have won in these types of lawsuits. See if you can speak to any of the clients of the attorney you are interviewing. Do this prior to making your final decision. If you cannot find a suitable attorney call the NAACP, Urban League, or other organizations involved in eliminating discrimination. They can refer you to qualified attorneys in your area.

It has been said that you should select an attorney as carefully as you would choose your spouse, business partners, doctor or financial advisor. Just as in any profession, there are good attorneys and bad ones. Not only must your attorney be qualified, they must have your best interests at heart. Avoid attorneys who are only concerned with how much money they will make and how quickly they will get paid.

Doing much of the legwork yourself is important. Provide your attorney with as much documentation and evidence as possible. You can share this work or compile all parties' documentation if you are involved in a class action suit. This will help reduce your attorney's time and legal fees. If you cannot afford an attorney, it is not a valid excuse for you to forfeit your legal rights. You have another option available. You have the legal right to represent yourself. When you represent yourself, they call it "In Pro Per."

Representing yourself requires that you become familiar with the appropriate state and federal laws, and court proceedings. You must learn how to process, respond to and file your legal papers. You must learn how to prepare and respond to interrogatories, depositions, subpoenas and court hearings. You must learn about court proceedings. Every state has law libraries and legal book stores. You can find the information that will teach you how to legally represent yourself. Librarians can also be extremely helpful. They can refer you to books and resources that will help you. Paralegal books and aids are also helpful. Learning the law takes a willingness to learn, time, effort and common sense. Common sense is a key factor. Consider the time you spend as an investment in your future.

While everyone cannot represent themselves, consider these facts. There are many non-attorneys who have been successful when representing themselves. They have won major complex legal cases. Some of these individuals never went to law school. Many of them never finished high school or entered college. They call them "jail house attorneys." Many of them are highly respected in the legal community by trial attorneys and judges. They are simply individuals who were willing to use their time and a law library to learn how to represent themselves. Many cities have legal "Do-It-Yourself" workshops" operated by attorneys. They charge reduced fees for assisting you in preparing your case or to review legal papers. These workshops are common today. You can find them in the Yellow Pages. Representing yourself "In Pro Per" is an option that cannot be ignored when you are unable to obtain an attorney. You can also file your case In Pro Per to avoided missing legal filing deadlines. Later you can hire an attorney to represent you.

Before you sue, file a complaint with one of the two federal government agencies which are responsible for handling discriminatory cases. They are the Department of Fair Employment and Housing (DFE&H) and the Equal Employment Opportunity Commission (EEOC). While you should file a complaint with these agencies, you should not expect them to satisfactorily resolve your job discrimination problem. It is easier for the DFE&H to determine and prove discrimination in housing than it is to identify and prove discrimination in employment. The DFE&H can use a simple test to determine if companies or individuals discriminate against minorities in housing. A simple test cannot be done to determine if employers discriminate in hiring and employment practices. Employers who discriminate are aware of this situation and take full advantage of it.

The EEOC received 70,339 complaints for the fiscal year ending September 1992. This was the second highest number of job discrimination complaints received in a fiscal year since the Civil Rights Acts became law in 1964. The only year to exceed this number of job discrimination complaints was 1988 (70,749). The average number of complaints is approximately 60,000 per year. Job discrimination complaints based on race continue to represent the largest number of complaints. In 1992 49.8 percent of the complaints were based on race. Sex discrimination complaints represented 29.8 percent of complaints. Approximately half of all complaints are received after an individual is fired. Settlements of $65.6 million were obtained in 1992. This is the second highest amount ever collected. Of this amount, $50.7 million was received for cases related to age discrimination suits.

While job discrimination complaints relating to race represented 49.8 percent of complaints in 1992, 77 percent of dollars ($50.7 million) collected was related to age discrimination. The remaining 23 percent of money collected (14.9 million dollars) was related to the remaining types of complaints including racial and sex discrimination complaints. These facts are clear indicators of how difficult it is to prove and receive compensation for racial employment discrimination when you depend solely on these agencies. Often you have to take additional legal steps. Usually these include filing a civil law suit to obtain justice or obtain compensation for your losses. You do this by obtaining a "right to sue letter" and an attorney to represent you.

Minorities complain about the DFE&H and the EEOC's inadequate performance when it comes to resolving racial employment discrimination complaints. These agencies can only handle clear-cut cases of discrimination. Most corporations are far too intelligent to openly discriminate. To further complicate these problems, over the years the DFE&H and the EEOC have been the recipients of major budget cuts. Most of these agencies do not have the staff, lawyers, time or money to properly investigate cases. Often it takes six months or longer before they can even start an investigation of your case.

One individual who was in the process of filing a complaint asked the agency's interviewer to make copies of his documentation for the agency's file. The interviewer explained she couldn't make the copies. She explained they had been out of copy paper for weeks because of budget cuts. She told him he would have to make copies and mail them to her. Minorities also said the agencies themselves discouraged them from filing employment complaints. These agencies are overwhelmed with case loads and cannot handle additional ones. It is a reality that these agencies cannot properly handle the large number of complaints they receive. Investigations are often limited to a few phone calls, letters and a request for documents. Too often they do not even interview witnesses or make on-site visits to companies. The actual investigation amounts to shuffling papers back and forth.

Agency personnel rarely speak with the plaintiff once they file the charge. The investigation ends up finding neither guilt nor innocence. If the plaintiff does not sue within one year after they filed the complaint, they lose their right to sue. Once they issue the individual "a right to sue letter," the agencies drop the case from their active files.

In light of this, most companies have little fear of the EEOC or DFE&H. They are fully aware that these agencies are understaffed, backlogged and restricted by budget cuts and limited personnel. Companies are experts at manipulating and circumventing discrimination laws. In fact they know how to manipulate discrimination laws so well that they can circumvent many agencies' standard investigations. This is one major reason why they continue to discriminate against minorities.

Minorities must be committed when they file complaints. If you have a valid discrimination complaint, don't let anyone talk you out of it. If you have to come back to speak with another person to file your complaint, do it. Ask to speak with a supervisor. Ask if other employees filed job discrimination suits. Try to start class action suits to strengthen your complaint.

Make sure you bring documentation and proof to support your complaints. This must include dates, names, witnesses and incidents. If you have no documents, explain your story in writing and show patterns which support your case. Ask witnesses in advance for their support and cooperation. If you feel the agency is not doing its job properly, write to the head of the agency, your member of Congress and state senator. Ask for their assistance. Be persistent; never give up.

Filing Your Complaint

Make sure your complaint is properly completed. Identify the forms of discrimination you encountered. If discriminated against in more than one area, list each area in your complaint. The areas of discrimination you encountered could be race, age and sex. If this is the case, each offense must be listed on your complaint. After you filed your complaint, you may be subjected to harassment or retaliation by your employer. If this happens, you will need to file additional charges with the DFE&H. Understanding there is legal time frames are important. You must file your complaint with these agencies and civil courts within the time frames required by law. If you do not, you will lose your right to file a complaint and to take legal action.

It is important to know that you have less time to file legal action for discrimination infractions than most other legal complaints. Generally, you must file your complaint with the DFE&H or EEOC within a year of the incident. You then must file your legal action (civil law suit) in federal or state courts within one year after the DFE&H & EEOC gives you the right to sue. Before you sue, obtain your "right to sue letter" from the DFE&H or EEOC. It allows you to request the court order defendant to reimburse you for legal fees if you win your case. Understanding you have specific time frames to exercise your legal options is important.

Worker's Compensation — Stress Leaves

In recent years many employees have been going on Worker's Compensation medical leaves due to stress. Your health is the most important asset you have. You must take the necessary steps to protect your health. You cannot live a quality life if you do not learn to manage and protect your health. Minorities and women must never use Worker's Compensation (medical stress leave) as a solution to discrimination. It is not the appropriate response. It will not rectify the problem and often creates additional problems when seeking future employment.

The stress that minorities and women experience is not due to incompetence or their lack of skills and abilities to succeed. Nor is it due to a lack of desire or an inability to handle the normal pressures of their careers. Often it is the direct result of unnecessary problems and frustrations associated with discrimination in their careers. It happens when they reach a point where they can no longer cope with discrimination. When this happens they lose the desire and will to function as professionals. This not only negatively affects their professional careers but their personal lives as well.

Medical stress leaves can have a negative impact on your future career. They become a negative and permanent part of your medical records. Employers are often unwilling or hesitant to hire employees who have taken medical stress leaves. They see this as risky. The most effective way to eliminate or reduce stress associated with discrimination is to address the problem in a proper manner. Learn not to become a victim. You become a victim when you allow others to damage your health and well-being. Minorities and women must learn how to empower themselves and protect their rights. Accomplish this by using the information in this book. Believe and have faith in yourself. Be willing to do the right thing.

Minorities and women must not allow the fear of losing their jobs prevent them from addressing discrimination. Never allow fear to prevent you from taking the right action. If fear is preventing you from addressing discrimination, use this empowering thought to take action:

"For God has not given us the spirit of fear, but of power, love, and a sound mind."

— *2nd Timothy chapter 1:8.*

We become mentally and physically fatigued and ill when we allow the frustrations of discrimination to build up and overwhelm us. This is guaranteed to happen when minorities and women fail to address discrimination. We must not become discouraged if we experience setbacks. Losing small skirmishes before winning the final victory is common.

Work to Improve the Future

Minorities must realize it is not only in their best interest but a matter of survival to use one of their most important assets. Unbelievably, they often discard this asset. This asset is their right to vote. Be aware of what's going on in the political arena. Be an active participant. The political climate has great influence on our lives. Minorities must be knowledgeable of which politicians have their best interests at heart. As stated earlier, the Department of Fair Employment and Housing and the Equal Employment Opportunity Commission have experienced drastic budget cuts. Minorities failed to supported politicians who fought for equality. We did not support them with our votes and did not keep them in office. If we did, these budget cuts may not have happened or could have been less drastic.

Minorities and women must take the time to learn about the political candidates running for office. We must know their positions on important issues, past voting records, what they have or have not supported in the past. We must provide support, whether in time or money, for all candidates who support racial and sexual equality. It is equally important that we work together to defeat political candidates who do not work to create parity in our society. Individuals or organizations who say they are working for a color-blind society but who are unwilling to work to eliminate the causes of racism are the reason it exists. Most important, we must be aware of individuals and organizations who threaten our civil rights. We must combat them on legal and moral grounds.

In California we have individuals such as Ward Connerly, Chairman of American Civil Rights Institute in Sacramento, and California Governor Pete Wilson who helped pass Proposition 209, the initiative that ended affirmative action in California. Ironically, Ward Connerly is a black man leading the fight against affirmative action. We must work together to remove they and their supporters from public office and prevent such people from obtaining office in the future.

Chapter Fifteen
VIABLE SOLUTIONS

America is woven of many strands; I would recognize them and let it so remain. . . . Our fate is to become one, and yet many —This is not prophecy, but description.

— Ralph Ellison

As long as the world shall last there will be wrongs, and if no man objected and no man rebelled, those wrongs would last forever.

— Clarence Darrow
Speech to jury, Chicago, Illinois, 1920

Like Life, racial understanding is not something that we must find, but something we must create. And so the ability of Negroes and whites to work together, to understand each other, will not be found ready-made; it must be created by the fact of contact.

— Martin Luther King, Jr.
The Words of Martin Luther King, Jr., *1987, p. 19*

This book has given its readers methods to detect and combat racism and sexism. It is my sincere desire that this book teach its readers that it is everyone's responsibility to eliminate the evil of discrimination. Accept this responsibility regardless of your race, color, creed, sex or title. It is not a matter of choice but a matter of survival to use this knowledge to ensure all individuals have equal opportunities in employment. Understanding the intent of this book is important. It is not to instill hate or distrust among minorities, non-minorities, and women. It is also not the intent of this book to create negative racial or sexual attitudes. The purpose of this book is to educate and inform its readers of the various forms of discrimination in the work place.

The purpose of this book is to eradicate prejudice and ignorance. It is to educate and enlighten people of all races and creeds about the negative effects of discrimination in American businesses. It is to show that it is in the best interest of our society to treat all individuals fairly.

Before you make a decision regarding someone of a different race or sex, ask yourself this question: How would you want that person to treat you if they were making the decision? Employers and minorities must develop a partnership to cultivate and develop lasting relationships. Relationships must be based on trust and a commitment to allow everyone an equal opportunity to succeed. The following recommendations will help accomplish this goal.

Establish Honest and Open Dialogue

Conditions that promote honest dialogue between minorities and their employers must be created. All parties must be allowed to express legitimate concerns and issues regarding employment discrimination without fear of retaliation or harassment. If employees identify legitimate problems, employers and co-workers must address them fairly.

> **"He who conceals his disease cannot expect to be cured."**
> **— African Proverb**

Creating New Corporate Cultures

Recognizing and promoting cultural diversity in the workplace can create positive change. This does not mean minorities should receive preferential treatment that would jeopardize the effectiveness of businesses or violate the rights of others. It means companies must be willing to take advantage of all the human resources available, regardless of race, sex, color or creed.

Corporations and businesses must appreciate the importance of cultural diversity. They must recognize it as an effective and acceptable way of doing business. It is essential that today's work force appropriately reflects the cultural diversity of the community and customers they serve. Corporations must be willing to take the time to understand different customs and ideologies of minority employees. This is important to employers because minorities and females represent more than 50 percent of today's work force.

This is confirmed in *Workforce 2000,* a study by the Department of Labor. It identifies the trends in the American work force. The current American work force consists of approximately 117.5 million workers. White men represent about 40 percent of the work force today and this number will be reduced by the year 2000. This also represents a major change in existing and potential customers. These new customers will purchase and use the products and services of businesses. Hiring token minorities or females will no longer be tolerable.

Just hiring African Americans, other minorities or female employees is not sufficient. This is examined in the article "Past Tokenism" (*Newsweek,* May 14, 1990): "Corporate America is beginning to realize that to make the most of nonwhite workers, it must move past hiring goals and tokenism and learn how to keep, motivate and promote minorities as well." Unfortunately, too many corporations fail to utilize this important idea. While corporations often make aggressive efforts to recruit African Americans, women and other minorities, their efforts have been ineffective. They fail to address the problems minorities and women endure. Their white co-workers are not accepting them as equal partners. Nor do employers do anything to ensure these minority groups can share equally in the success and rewards of their efforts and contributions.

This results in minorities leaving companies just as fast as they are hired. Corporations must be willing to examine the reasons why many talented minorities are leaving their companies. This shows the importance of employers conducting minority employees' exit interviews. Employers must be willing to ask minorities why they are leaving. Employers must be willing to address the important concerns of minority employees.

"Past Tokenism" made other useful suggestions to corporations wanting to effectively promote and use diversity in the work place. The article recommended hiring consultants to conduct diversity seminars. These include teaching management and managers how to overcome and eliminate subtle biases that have negative impact on the support, performance and the perceptions of minority employees. These types of training are valuable. The article showed how white managers are enlightened and sometimes embarrassed after discovering their biased beliefs, such as the view that articulate black executives are exceptions, while intelligence in whites is normal. Biased beliefs such as these create and perpetuate discrimination and racism, whether intentional or not.

When white employees believe black employees are inferior, they have almost no trust or confidence in their abilities or opinions. White employees with these beliefs will not provide challenging assignments to black employees. This impedes their professional growth due to lack of experience and exposure. Another valuable technique used by consultants and psychologists is "labeling" and "role playing." It gives employees a unique perspective and is effective in helping individuals to understand and eliminate biased opinions. When used properly, it will create better working relationships and promote cultural diversity in the work place. This technique shows how labels are attached to individuals based on their race, customs, sex, positions, and other differences.

Labeling shows how employees are treated based on preconceived opinions (labels). Groups of employees are selected. Large labels with a specific characteristic (genius, fools, confident, president, militant, etc.) are secured to each employee's forehead. They are not allowed to see the label placed on their own foreheads. Each individual in the group is now told to interact with each other for a few minutes. Individuals will react to each other according to the labels they see on each other's foreheads. Each person is treated according to their label instead of the true merits or faults of each individual. The way each individual is treated will affect the way that individual responds to others in the group. For example, the group will treat the person labeled as president with respect and authority. He or she will in turn respond to others as a person of authority. The group will treat the individual labeled as a fool as if his or her opinion does not matter. Soon the individual labeled as a fool will not feel comfortable expressing his or her opinions. This person keeps his or her opinions to them self. The individual labeled as a fool will not fit into the group. This exercise shows employees how they can incorrectly relate to others based on unfounded opinions (labels). It shows how this adversely affects a person's feelings, responses and performance.

Minorities represent an important segment of the work force. It is irresponsible and a sign of a lack of commitment when businesses fail to investigate why they are unable to retain or promote talented minority and female employees. Corporations must not wait until after valuable minorities leave. They must develop procedures to monitor and follow up on the progress of new and long-term minority employees. This is the only way to ensure they treat them equally. Employers must take a proactive approach as opposed to a reactive approach. As the old saying goes, "An ounce of prevention is worth more than a pound of cure."

Corporations must be willing to treat their employees as valuable assets. This can be accomplished by developing internal minority review programs and open forums to monitor the progress of minority employees. These programs and forums can consist of training classes, seminars, questionnaires, and open discussion. Companies must utilize the valuable information they provide by using it to adjust to the changing diverse work force.

Using the services of outside consulting firms may initially appear expensive but can result in major savings in the long run. They can be highly effective in training management and employees to adapt to the cultural diversity of the workplace. This can result in lower employee turnover and reduced legal fees. It will also result in greater productivity and harmony in the workplace. Consultants can train staff to effectively work with a diverse work force, and develop mentor and minority training programs. They work with employers to show them how to create parity in the work place. When cost is a major concern, video and audio tape training programs can be purchased or rented at reasonable prices.

Another problem is the deterioration of the moral and professional ethics in the corporate environment. Too many companies have developed "kill or be killed," or "get them before they get you" philosophy. Senior level management encourages this attitude which has led to the downfall of many companies. They may achieve some levels of short-term success, but will fail over the long term. This type of attitude leads employees to believe the only way they can succeed is to take advantage of others. These employees believe that doing anything to succeed is appropriate. They are willing to do this at the expense of employees, customers, and their employers. This leads employees to believe it is appropriate to intentionally sabotage other employees' success, lie, cheat and steal. These employees show a willingness to harm others even when it is not necessary and inappropriate.

Companies should conduct annual mandatory classes on the importance of ethics in business and human relationships. Ethics classes should teach management and employees that an attitude of winning at all costs can result in tragic repercussions for employees and their employers.

Ethics classes should include explanations of how discrimination, lying, cheating, and sabotaging other success harms everyone. These types of classes help build moral character, unity, trust, and respect for all employees. They result in positive contributions from all employees instead of a small segment of the work force. Companies' ethical and anti-discrimination philosophies must not be limited to two-hour workshops or employee orientations. They must become part of the daily working environment and have the full support of senior-level management.

When designed properly and companies are sincere, these programs are effective tools in creating understanding, communication, equality, and harmony among all employees. This creates an atmosphere of high employee morale and increased productivity. Good business ethics are the keys to increasing long-term profits for corporations. They promote high productivity, quality goods and services, a positive company image and valuable contributions to the communities they serve.

Establish Written Plans

Successful businesses create business plans for ten-, five- and one-year periods. They establish goals and time frames, monitor progress, and hold responsible parties accountable. These techniques insure companies and corporations are sincere in creating parity in the workplace. Written affirmative action plans and guidelines should not be considered options but mandatory tools in dismantling discrimination.

Affirmative action goals must be specific, measurable, and identifiable. They must be company policies which are enforced. All employees must be made aware of them to ensure they achieve them. These written goals must be monitored to ensure they are being accomplished. Employers must immediately take appropriate corrective actions when the goals are not being achieved. This must be a company priority.

Fair and equitable methods must be used to mediate disputes. When review or investigative committees are established they must include appropriate minority representation. Committees must have the power to make decisions, take actions, and discipline individuals regardless of their positions. When it is inappropriate for company personnel to make decisions, independent mediators should be brought in to investigate and resolve complaints.

We Must Eliminate Our Trade Deficit

In chapter eight we discussed how our foreign trade deficits are responsible for the loss of jobs and unemployment. Regardless of your race or nationality, you must become a concerned and informed citizen and consumer. Make sure the companies you patronize don't just carry products that are manufactured outside the United States. Learn where they manufactured their products before you buy them. Take the time to read labels or ask questions. It only takes a few extra seconds.

Make your concerns known to political representatives. Before you vote for candidates know, their past and present position on the trade deficit. Take the time to review their records on this issue. Insist that they support laws that will properly reduce the trade deficit. Make sure they will work to reduce lobbyists' influence. Work to defeat politicians who support and lobby for unfair foreign trade practices. Inform your family and friends. Get involved in political groups that address these issues. Make them aware of your concerns. Learn and teach others the important facts about this problem.

Today there are major concerns concerning the North America Free Trade Agreement (NAFTA). Does this agreement improve or increase our trade deficit? Does it add to the depletion of American jobs and businesses or create new ones? This agreement was passed in November 1993 and few Americans took the time to learn how it affects them. Most Americans failed to decide or take action to support or defeat this agreement.

When many Americans decided to take action, it was based on what other individuals told them. The American work force must play a more active role in government decisions that will have an impact on future jobs. Do this by calling your member of Congress. Become actively involved in legislation so your voice is known. Do this regardless if it is for or against legislation. This is important because these types of legal agreements will have major impacts on the lives of American workers and our country's future.

One final thought on this topic. It is not good business to buy goods and services just because they are produced in America. As Americans, we have a responsibility to produce and provide quality goods and services. We must be committed to producing the best products on the market. Americans must take pride in their work. Americans must learn from past mistakes. An excellent example of this is the American automobile industry. In the past this industry allowed the quality of their cars to deteriorate. They designed cars that looked good but performed poorly and did not last. This resulted in consumers' loss of confidence in American cars.

Consumers became dissatisfied with inferior American-made cars. They began to purchase foreign cars which were better built. The American Automobile industry suffered major losses and it took years to rebuild their image and gain customers' confidence. Today, American cars are better or just as good as any other cars made in the world. Produce the best goods, provide the best services and your customers will seek you out even if they have to pay a premium. Have pride in your work. Provide goods and services that you would like to receive. Never strive for the quick and easy profit. Take the time to work to develop long-term relationships and customer loyalty.

Other Recommendations

- Establish mentor programs for minorities and women

- Educational opportunities for minorities and women managerial candidates

- Create incentive and reward programs to encourage participation in company-wide anti-discrimination training and education programs

- Develop training and work-study programs which include minority employees. The programs' purposes are to obtain and maintain the skills needed for current and new technological market demands.

- Create and support proactive intervention programs to deal with complaints of racism and sexism. Employers must be willing to act against employees (despite their positions) who discriminate. Minority employees must not be punished for valid complaints or identifying discriminatory practices. They must feel confidant that their complaints will be taken seriously and acted upon.

- Establish employee and management counseling programs that teach employees how to address and eliminate racism and bigotry in the workplace.

- Instruct executives and senior management to become directly involved in eliminating racism and discrimination in the workplace.

- Establish minority internship and work-study programs; liaise with public schools to provid young people with positive work experiences.

- Create and support community outreach programs to assist underprivileged children. These children will have either a positive or negative impact on the future of our country. This will be determined by the type and amount of assistance that we provide to them.

- Prepare and encourage minorities and women to apply for advanced positions. Minority and women employees must in turn let their employers know they want the opportunity to obtain higher level positions.

- Lobby politicians for more effective anti-discriminatory employment laws. These must include severe penalties that are incentives not to discriminate. The government must provide the means to enforce the laws. They must change discriminatory laws because they place an unfair burden on minorities to prove their cases in court. They must provide adequate funding and manpower to government departments such as the EEOC and DFHE. This is the only way they can properly investigate discriminatory complaints and take appropriate actions. These agencies must be able to investigate and resolve complaints on a timely basis.

Strategies

Companies have major advantages. They control and have access to personnel files and records of discrimination complaints and minority grievances. Usually, minorities do not have access to this type of information. Companies will not make these records available to the public and to employees. They believe it is to their advantage to suppress this information. Because of this, it is important that minorities maintain their own records and files on discrimination complaints. One way to accomplish this as an employee is to conduct your own independent and unbiased survey. You can do this by preparing your own questionnaires and circulating them among minority employees.

This can be a great source of useful information. Try to contact former employees. They may have had grievances. When possible obtain copies of letters, reports and other pertinent information. Develop your own files and records. Keep records on how they resolved complaints. Develop your own statistical data. All this information is vital evidence. It can be the deciding factor in winning your case in court.

Another method is to circulate petitions to substantiate proof of discrimination and a consensus of support from minority employees. This also makes information general knowledge. When done properly, it is persuasive. Petitions can also be evidence. It is important to be aware that these types of procedures should be done off company property and not during working hours. Contact your co-workers at home or at off-site locations and be just as effective. You will have better results if this is done off-site and in a friendly environment.

Learn how to work with other minorities to accomplish your goals. You will find that often they want to achieve the same goals you desire. Develop forums and network with other minority groups. Establish multinational organizations within your corporation. You will find corporations are more responsive to organized groups as opposed to a single individual. We must stop voting for candidates because they are the same race. We must vote for our representatives based on their commitment to issues. We also need to know which candidates are willing to help their constituents on issues that are of concern to you and other minorities.

Therefore, I cannot over emphasize the importance of political power. When used properly it bestows unlimited benefits upon minorities. When political power is not properly utilized or is wasted, the results are often catastrophic to the lives and opportunities of African Americans and other minorities.

Chapter Sixteen

PERSONAL REFLECTIONS

To an unrecognized extent, we're a nation of professional, religious, ethnic and racial tribes — the Tribes of America — who maintain a fragile truce, easily and often broken. We had to conquer this continent — and its original tribes — in order to exploit its resources. But we were never able to conquer our atavistic hatreds, to accept our widely diverse pasts, to transcend them, to live together as a single people.

> *— Paul Cowan*
> The Tribes of America, *1979*

A man who will not labor to gain his rights, is a man who would not, if he had them, prize and defend them.

> *— Frederick Douglass*

A doctrine of black supremacy is as evil as a doctrine of white supremacy.
> *— Martin Luther King, Jr.*
> The Words of Martin Luther King, Jr., *p. 19*

No person in their right mind enjoys or looks forward to challenging discriminatory practices with their employer. This takes tremendous courage and commitment. It requires a willingness to place your principles first and your job or career second. Most individuals would never think of jeopardizing their jobs or careers for their principles or values. These same people are guaranteed to never succeed or find personal fulfillment in their professions or lives. We pay a terrible price when we allow fear to prevent us from supporting our values.

To have a successful and rewarding professional life, know the difference between a job and a career. A job is something we do to receive payment for our services. It is not something we have a passion for or enjoy doing. Minorities and women must learn to seek careers not jobs. This must be done if we are serious about achieving success and fulfillment in our professions and lives. A career must allow you the opportunity to advance as far as your abilities, talents and desires will take you. A career is defined as "a chosen pursuit, profession or occupation. It is the general course or progression of one's life (especially in a profession). It is a path or course one chooses. It is a moment of the highest pitch or peak" (*American Heritage Dictionary*).

The verb "career" means to move or run at full speed ahead. No one can have a successful career when they allow others to limit their success intentionally or unintentionally. It violates the meaning and intention of the word career. We cannot achieve happiness in our career when we allow others to force us to forfeit our rights as human beings. We cannot feel good about ourselves when we allow others to unfairly control and limit our careers. When we allow others to impede this basic principle, it decays the values that sustain our lives.

With today's concern for happiness, health and longevity people are wisely concerned about healthy eating habits. We understand we are what we eat. Poor eating habits adversely affect the quality of our lives. They are the source of health problems, lack of energy, and poor concentration. They cause premature death. We must properly feed our careers and personal lives, too. To succeed our decisions and actions must be based on sound principles and values. Our principles and values are the fuel (food) that sustain our emotional, physical and spiritually lives. We must possess the convictions and mental fortitude to support our values and principles even when faced with difficult decisions.

These qualities give meaning and substance to our lives. All great men and women of substance possess these qualities. They are the ingredients that allow individuals to endure extreme difficulties and the courage to die for their beliefs. This special quality allows them to add value to the lives of everyone they meet. Martin Luther King Jr., and others died trying to achieve racial equality in America. During and after their lives they raised the moral consciousness of our country. We dishonor him and others like him by not continuing their work. Each of us, regardless of our race or sex has a responsibility to continue this important work.

To attain a rewarding and satisfying life, we must identify, create, and nurture important values and beliefs. Adversity is what adds value to our lives. We grow as individuals when we overcome adversity. Unfortunately, most people never realize this. They allow adversity to consume them. Minorities must understand that the constant emotional stress and backlash from ignoring discrimination are life threatening. It makes them more susceptible to cancer, high blood pressure, heart attacks and other physical illnesses.

As earlier stated there is great emphasis on proper diet and exercise to maintain good health. This is important but minorities must be aware of another important factor in the equation for good health and longevity. Often the primary reasons for minorities' poor health, sicknesses and premature deaths are not caused by what they eat or don't eat. It is not because of their lack of exercise. They are caused by "what's eating at them."

When we allow our jobs, fears, frustrations, and feelings of hopelessness control our lives, they devour our spirit. Our spirit is the driving force in our lives. Without it we cannot function as human beings. We are eaten alive from the inside out. This is a painful slow death. One small bite after another. This occurs when we forfeit our dreams, dignity, pride, self respect, values and principles. We lose the capacity to believe in ourselves and to succeed. This is a slow and tortuous death. We see and feel ourselves dying before our very eyes.

The problems become more severe because we pass on this sense of hopelessness and pain to our children. This is a burden and a painful experience for any adult. It is even more devastating to our children. It is a horrible thought for anyone to exist in this manner. Instead of living our lives this way, we must seek effective solutions. It starts by not waiting for someone else to do something. Accept this responsibility and your quality of life will improve a hundredfold.

Accepting responsibility requires you to pay a price. It can result in losing a frustrating and limiting job. It may cause some financial difficulties. But this change can also establish new, rewarding careers, and financial independence never dreamed possible. Empowering yourself will cause you to lose mediocre associates. It will also lead you to new empowering and supportive friends for life. You will encounter emotional traumas that lead to personal growth that enriches your life.

"No matter how long the night the day is sure to come."
— African Proverb

If you study the lives of successful people, you will find they never achieved success without personal sacrifices. You will never find success if you fail to address the challenges that impede your career. Success does not happen overnight. We must learn patience and not become frustrated when we make important changes in our lives. Never allow yourself to become discouraged or to quit, because success takes time.

Les Brown, a motivational speaker and author, related the story of the Chinese bamboo tree in one of his speeches. It is the perfect metaphor to illustrate this important point. The Chinese bamboo tree must be watered and nurtured daily. It takes about five years before the sprouts reach the topsoil. Within five weeks after the sprouts reach the topsoil the tree grows to 90 feet. It takes five years to see the results of one's efforts and hard work. The results and benefits appeared in five short weeks once the process is near completion. This is a valuable life lesson. Our hard work, faith, and vision must sustain us during difficult times. We must continue to persevere when we don't see the results or reap the rewards of our efforts.

Success in our careers and personal lives is created by establishing worthwhile goals. This requires developing effective plans to achieve our goals and overcoming barriers that prevent us from achieving them. Minorities automatically forfeit theirs dreams, visions and goals when they try to ignore obstacles which prevent success. I personally experienced this when I was employed with a Fortune 100 company. The company was insensitive toward the rights of African Americans and other minorities. Initially I tried to ignore the discriminatory culture and atmosphere. I tried to make the most of a bad situation by wearing blinders. It morally bankrupted my career, health, and life. It became progressively worse until it was unbearable. I became empty inside and died a thousand deaths. I discovered the more I ignored discriminatory activities, the more difficult the situation became.

Employees and companies that participate in discrimination against others see "green lights flashing and full-steam ahead signs" whenever victims fail to confront discrimination. I endured racial discrimination for five years before I confronted my employer. Out of fear, I procrastinated. Due to years of emotional and physical abuse from discrimination I became distraught. For the next two years I confronted racial discriminatory practices engaged in by my employer.

When I addressed the company about these practices, I was subjected to harassment and retaliation. I was forced to resign for my physical and emotional well-being. I continued my fight against racial discrimination with my employer by pursuing legal action. After several years, the matter was "mutually resolved." I have several regrets regarding this experience. My first regret is that it happened. My second regret is that I waited five years before I had the courage to confront discriminatory activities. In my case legal action was necessary. Hopefully by using the information in this book legal action will be unnecessary. This book was written because of my experience and to help eliminate racism, bigotry and sexism in the workplace and in our society.

Being the constant victim of discrimination makes anyone lose passion for their profession and the career they once loved. Instead of being fulfilled, minorities become frustrated, resentful and bitter toward their work and others. This has an adverse effect on minorities' abilities to perform by creating negative attitudes. If minorities fail to properly address discrimination, it will adversely affect them the rest of their lives.

This experience taught me an invaluable lesson I will never forget. I made this statement earlier in this book. It is so important it warrants being repeated and memorized. It is an idea that minorities and non minorities must understand, believe in and practice. It is the only way discrimination will be eliminated. We must ask ourselves two important questions. When and how should we address discrimination? The correct answer is a simple one. Address discrimination whenever it occurs. Never use the excuse "I am waiting for the right opportunity" as justification to ignore discrimination. When we choose to wait, we not only give our permission but endorse discrimination as an acceptable way of life. Whenever we address discrimination, we must respond with integrity, intelligence, honesty, common sense, and with the spirit of God in our hearts. Only by doing this can we successfully eliminate discrimination in corporate America and the workplace.

As I previously stated, I was the victim of racial discrimination by a former employer. This was not an isolated experience at this corporation. Other highly qualified, dedicated, professional African Americans and other minorities experienced identical problems. Several filed complaints and others filed legal actions against the company. This book is dedicated to them and all other minorities and women who are victims of discrimination.

Female employees have traditionally been victims of sex discrimination by employers. Companies must be receptive to their needs in our ever changing society. With the divorce rate at more than 52 percent, and the growing trend of single mothers, women face challenges that are foreign to men. They include sole responsibility of child care. This is a full-time job. This obligation becomes more challenging when women are paid less than male employees for identical work.

Companies must accept the challenge of addressing women's concerns.

The success and survival of corporations will depend on how well they accomplish this goal. Women are a vital segment of today's work force. Employers cannot ignore their issues without disastrous repercussions. Progressive and innovative companies have successfully met this challenge. They found the talents of women lucrative to their companies. Businesses have discovered that by allowing women equal participation in the work force they experienced extra benefits, including a new surge of employee dedication and happier, healthier, more productive employees. They found this improved performance in both male and female workers. It accomplished this by stimulating employee competitiveness within the entire work force. This happens when they judge employees on their performance and potential, and rewards are equally obtainable. Employees are more productive when they are not judged by their gender. This results in increased profits and company performance.

This can be achieved without putting corporations at risk. This has been accomplished by allowing employees to be more productive and eliminating unnecessary stress in their lives. Simple things such as providing equal opportunities and pay to women and implementing flex hours, allowing employees to work at home, providing on-site day care for children, and allowing extended child care leave has provided enormous benefits to employers and employees. These accommodations make the difference between success and failure for employees and the companies they serve.

It is a sad commentary that mothers who want to work cannot afford to work. They are restricted by antiquated laws which prevent them from working while receiving limited public assistance. These mothers can receive more money, health care, and other public assistance for themselves and their children by staying at home. If they obtain jobs, they forfeit all public assistance. Often the only jobs they can obtain do not pay enough to cover child care and other necessities. This prevents many mothers from obtaining the work experience and training needed to acquire higher-paying jobs. This problem is no longer limited to uneducated and unskilled mothers; professional mothers are experiencing the same problems.

It's been said that prostitution is the oldest profession and there is a valid reason for it: "It is a silly question to ask a prostitute why she does it. . . . These are the highest-paid 'professional' women in America" (Gail Sheehy, *Hustling,* 1971).

The lack of quality jobs for women are major contributors to drugs and prostitution. "Whether our reformers admit it or not, the economic and social inferiority of women is responsible for prostitution" (Emma Goldman, "The Traffic in Women," *Anarchism and Other Essays*).

> "A girl should not expect special privileges because of her sex, but neither should she 'adjust' to prejudice and discrimination. She must learn to compete then, not as a woman, but as a human being."
> — *India* *Edwards,* **Pulling** **No Punches,**

When companies adjust to the needs of women employees they must not regard it as special treatment or a burden. They must look upon it as good business sense. Women must be allowed to compete on an equal playing field.

In Hillary Rodham Clinton's 1995 address to the United Nations Conference on Women in Beijing, she said, "Much of the work we do is not valued — not by economists, not by historians, not by popular culture, not by government leaders." This is put in proper perspective when we look at how women's earnings have been spiraling downward in recent years. In 1979 women earnings were 62 percent of men's average earnings; this grew to 76.8 percent by 1993, but decreased to 76.4 percent in 1994, and is predicted to decrease dramatically in the next several years.

Before I end this book, I would like to share several personal experiences. Companies' outward appearances are generally cordial and friendly. Pleasant outward appearances and smiles are often deceptive. They are often used to hide and/or perpetuate discrimination. Do not be misled by them.

Corporate America often has management that habitually discriminates against African Americans, other minorities and women. This happens even when management appears friendly and kind. They are polite and always ready with a smile or friendly word. Minorities must be very suspicious of superficial appearances. Beneath this facade are individuals who are committed to depriving them of their civil rights. I experienced first hand outward friendly postures which were deceptive from executives, middle and lower management. One such experience happened with a vice president of human resources. We met after I wrote a letter to the company president. It explained minorities were subjected to serious

> "He may say that he loves you. Wait and see what he does for you."
> — *African* *Proverb*

discriminatory problems throughout the corporation. The letter stated the problems, including denial of promotional opportunities, unequal pay, and biased performance evaluations, all based on race. The letter also explained how minorities were being harassed and intentionally set up for failure. The letter informed the president that these issues were previously brought to management's attention and nothing had been done.

The president referred this matter the vice president of human resources. He gave her the power to act on his authority to investigate the matter. She was extremely pleasant and friendly. Her smile placed me at ease. During our meetings she went out of her way to make me feel comfortable. She expressed concern about the problems minorities were experiencing. She was receptive to my ideas and recommendations. Our meeting always ended with her promising to investigate the problems we discussed. This contrived sense of concern lured me into a false sense of security. This allowed the company to take advantage of me and other minorities.

During meetings she always sidestepped tough questions. Meetings were spread over several months. But nothing was ever resolved. They made no changes; nothing happened to managers who were discriminating against minorities. When answers were provided, they were non-responsive and meaningless. The only change was to make my job unbearable.

The vice president of human resources was part of the problem. She never intended to address the issues of racial discrimination. She was aware other long-term minority employees had filed discrimination complaints. They wrote them before I wrote my letter. She never met or spoke with them. This happened because she had no concern for their problems. The employees never resolved their problems. They were all forced to leave the company. The vice president met with me only because I wrote a letter to the president. It would look inappropriate if there was no official response to my letter. In fact, the president never gave me the professional courtesy of speaking or meeting with me. He never contacted me or followed up to see how I was doing. The president's office was in the same building two floors above mine. The president just assigned the matter to the vice president of human resources.

During our first meeting I expressed concerns the company would retaliate against me for writing my letter. The vice president gave me her and the president's word no one would retaliate. Within five months they demoted me and forced to me hire employees against my will. I was systematically set up for failure, humiliated, and written-up on several occasions.

These actions forced me to write a letter to the president of the parent corporation. I asked him to investigate this matter. He assigned it to a vice president of human resources from the corporate office. He was responsible for investigating my complaint. He also appeared friendly and concerned. He asked me to give him the names of other employees who experienced discrimination. I provided the names. After a three-day investigation he concluded no discrimination existed. He stated the only problem he found was me. I was at fault and discrimination did not exist.

During his investigation he conducted private, one-on-one meetings with employees of his choice. He only chose to speak with one other black employee, who also complained about discrimination. He refused to meet with the other black employees who had complained. He would not meet them individually or as a group. He refused to listen to their complaints. He never met with one of the company's former top salesman, a black man who had recently written a letter about racial discrimination he had experienced in the company.

This vice president's actions also showed he was not concerned about protecting minority rights. During and after this investigation they harassed me and retaliated against me. They moved me from my office to one that was unsuitable for habitation. The temperature controls did not work in this room because of a building design flaw. It had been used as a storage room prior to my moving in. I was forced to remove storage boxes and clean the room prior to moving in. This was humiliating. I was a manager and was forced to act in the capacity of a janitor. This room was extremely cool in the morning and so hot in the afternoon I could not work in it. They took my computer from me. They excluded me from meetings, making it impossible for me to do my work. They no longer allowed me to hire my supervisors. They denied me the opportunity to transfer to other departments. These are just some of the indignities I was forced to endure after my complaint.

Within a year all of the black employees whose names I had given to the vice president had been forced out or fired. So much for the impartial investigation and the protection promised to me by the president and two vice presidents. The most frightening thing about my experience was the similarity of their responses. On the surface they seemed fair, concerned, and friendly. But they all failed to address the problems. When corporations are not committed to eliminating racial discrimination, receiving fair treat-

> "A fox should not be on the jury at a goose's trial."
> —*Thomas Fuller.*

ment is impossible for minorities. These corporations cannot conduct unbiased internal discriminatory investigations.

As I previously stated, I was unable to amicably resolve the problems with my employer and was forced to resign. I exercised my final option and pursued legal recourse.

Another incident occurred during the deposition for my lawsuit filed against my former employer. When asked by their attorney if I experienced discrimination at other jobs. I explained it only happened once. An employer wrote a untrue, derogatory article about their black employees in the company's magazine. I later realized I unintentionally gave a wrong answer. Minorities are conditioned to overlook and deny the existence of discrimination and racism when subjected to it. They conditioned me to ignore it. They taught me to hope conditions would improve by themselves. It is a safety mechanism minorities create to survive the constant bombardment of discrimination and racism.

My response was incorrect because discrimination and racism are prevalent in this country. It is so frequent that minorities come to view it as the normal way of doing business. Minorities avoid labeling bigotry as "discrimination and racism." These words are too painful to endure. Discrimination and racism make minorities feel like hopeless victims. They make minorities feel they are of little value and have no control over their lives. They program minorities to see "discrimination and racism" in terms of bad luck and imaginary deficiencies in their abilities. In the past, minorities avoided seeing discriminatory incidents as racism because they had been conditioned to believe it's wrong to think this way. They were conditioned to believe they should be happy to have a job, regardless how badly they were treated. Minorities also knew they would be committing "professional suicide" if they approached employers about discriminatory practices. They know from experience they would be labeled as trouble makers and forfeit any hopes of achieving a successful career with their employer.

All black men have experienced racism in our country. They have difficulty verbally expressing and sharing the pain and frustrations they experience from racism. This problem is explored in *Essence* magazine, a special men's edition, November 1992. In the article "Racism, The Hurt That Men Won't Name," psychologist Howard Mabry is quoted: "Men tend to be task-oriented; they tend to think of solutions rather than just express feelings. They must learn just to talk, to vent feelings." The article also explained,

"The war of the nineties is a 'cold' war; there are no more 'whites only' signs visible and the rules have changed. The enemy itself is often invisible — a faceless voice on the telephone, a glass ceiling that lets you rise only so far, a villain like the creature in the movie *Predator* — unseen but fatally felt."

Reflecting on my past, I now realized I experienced racial discrimination from my early work experience as a child throughout my adult life. In my early teens I was not allowed to deliver newspapers in white neighborhoods because I was black. In high school I worked after school in a hospital for years without any hopes of advancement — black males worked in lower level jobs for years and were never promoted. It did not matter how well they performed. They promoted attractive black women only if they became sexually involved with white male managers.

Working full time at another company during college, I recall that black students were repeatedly passed over for promotions. They quickly promoted new white employees we trained that had less education and experience. During my professional career I had to work harder than my white counterparts to be promoted. I received less assistance and had less authority than white counterparts. I knew no matter how good my work was it was unlikely I would advance beyond middle management positions.

Early in my career I had such a horrible experience with racism, I blocked it out of my mind for years. I was once offered a management job only because I was black and because there had been legal action against the company for their discriminatory hiring practices. I had unknowingly been hired as the token black manager. I moved three thousand miles to accept this position. I had been told I would be the manager of an accounting department. When I started, I was given the title of manager but in reality I had no authority, duties or responsibilities.

I worked for about a month without having anything really substantial to do. When I discussed this discriminatory practice with senior management, they told me that white long-term employees were unwilling to report to a black manager. They had threatened to quit if I was made their supervisor. Management also informed me they were required by law to hire black managers. They then stated the law did not require them to give minorities challenging work or managerial responsibilities. They were only required to hire and pay them. They told me it would take years for white employees to accept black managers. They told me that I should enjoy this opportunity to make easy money. I resigned from the company after that meeting. I was not looking for a free ride. I was looking to gain valuable experience. I wanted to make important contributions to the company I worked for.

Later in my career, I experienced problems with a senior manager who was engaged in activities that were violating company policy. Because of the severe nature of the problem, I was forced to take it up with his superiors. I was a manager, but because I was black, the company failed to intercede for me. I knew if I had been white the problem would have been corrected immediately.

I did not think of these and other experiences during the deposition. This is how minorities are normally treated in their professional careers. To survive the mental anguish such treatment causes, blacks suppress these unpleasant experiences from their conscious minds. Blacks know this phenomenon as "stay-in-your-place" racism. "Stay-in-your-place racism abides by the law of limits — that unspoken policy that limits a black man's access to power" (*Essence* 1992, "Racism, The Hurt That Men Won't Name").

It must be made clear that there are many outstanding companies that produce excellent goods and services, and are committed to treating minorities fairly. Unfortunately, the inappropriate practices of others smear them. The companies who treat minorities fairly work with minorities not just to help minorities but to improve their performance as well. This results in positive benefits for businesses and contributes to their long-term success.

Despite the difficulties I encountered, I know I did the right thing by pursuing legal action. I initially experienced financial and other difficulties because of this experience. I also received financial rewards, personal and professional satisfaction. This book was written to share this knowledge and to help others. It was written to expose discriminatory practices and to show how detrimental they are to employers and employees.

This book was written as therapy to comfort other minorities who suffered from the evils of discrimination. It was written to provide hope and inspiration to others. It is my sincere desire that it will inspire corporations, companies and individuals to make positive changes in their policies and their lives. This book was not written to hurt individuals or America businesses. It was written in the hopes that it would be a positive catalyst for voluntary change. This change will not only improve our society but the quality of all of our lives, regardless of our race, sex, color or creed. This can be accomplished when we understand that discrimination is a detriment to everyone's success. It becomes easier to eliminate discrimination when we know the facts and destroy the myths that perpetuate discrimination.

This book was written to prepare minorities' children to cope with the inequities they will encounter in their lives because of their race.

> You will tell your children this world is wrong. But, because that world is there, they will have to struggle to survive, with scales weighted against them. They will have to work harder and do better, yet the result may be less recognition and reward. We all know life can be unfair. For black people, this knowledge is not an academic theory but a fact of daily life"
>
> — Andrew Hacker,
> *Two Nations Black and White,*
> *Separate, Hostile, Unequal* , p. 34

While this book was written to expose the harsh realities of discrimination in the work place, discrimination goes far beyond our places of employment. Racism and discrimination have been institutionalized in many segments of our society. It not only exists in employment but in our educational system, our legal system, our government, and daily activities we encounter. They are a reflection of our society's beliefs.

Five years after the brutal beating of Rodney King on March 4, 1991, the news media and public are still debating the impact of the video showing the savage police assault on Rodney King. Many were outraged, while others believed it was justified. Minorities must recognize that the actions of four police officers and selected others are not valid reasons to condemn all police. African Americans must understand that there are good and bad individuals in all professions. Police are necessary and vital to our communities. Without police our society would be in chaos. Police risk their lives daily and sometimes sacrifice their lives to protect us. We must respect their authority when it is within the bounds of the law.

They initially acquitted the four white police officers on all charges on April 29, 1992. Eventually two (Theodore Briseno and Timothy Wind) were acquitted, while two (Stacey Koon and Laurence Powell) were found guilty in a second federal trial, each receiving three-year prison terms. Everyone recognizes the names of the four white police officers, Sergeant Stacey Koon, Laurence Powell, Theodore Briseno, Timothy Wind. We knew and recognized their names worldwide.

On the same day they acquitted the four police officers, a small percentage of the Los Angeles blacks, Hispanic, and white population were involved in rioting. They assaulted innocent bystanders and looted and burned property in protest or for personal gain. But the news media slanted their news coverage to make it appear that only blacks were rioting. *The State of Black America 1993* describes a much more accurate picture of the facts and realities of the 1992 Los Angeles riots:

> And while Los Angeles is thought of as an explosion of African-American protest, it actually was America's first interracial, multi-cultural riot. More Latinos than blacks were arrested, and one of every seven people taken into custody by the police was white — a reminder that white racism condemns disproportionate numbers of African Americans to lives of poverty and despair; anger based on economic inequality cuts across racial and ethnic lines (p. 3)."

Television stations broadcast live coverage of the riots and live footage of Reginald Denny being dragged from his truck and brutally beaten by four blacks. This incident became the main focus of the coverage of the Los Angeles riots by the news media. Four African Americans were arrested and prosecuted for the incident. Their names were publicized daily for more than a year — Damian Monroe Williams, Henry Keith Watson, Gary Williams, and Antoine Eugene Miller. The Rodney King and Reginald Denny trials not only polarized Los Angeles but citizens around the world. The news media devoted much of their coverage to the negativity of the riots. The criminal prosecution of the four police officers and the four black defendants charged with beating Reginald Denny was front-page news for years.

Regardless of whether you are black, white, Hispanic, or Asian, we must realize that the beating of Rodney King and Reginald Denny were wrong. We cannot tolerate such behavior in our society. To address this problem, we must understand imprisoning criminals will not solve the problem. Their numbers have already overwhelmed our society and will continue to increase, and in any case they will eventually be released. America has become a society in which its number one commodity is the mass production of discrimination, racism, poverty, unemployment and violence. The correct solution to this dilemma is not to attack the symptoms. We must concentrate our efforts on eliminating the root of the problem. The roots of the problem are racism, discrimination, poverty, inadequate education and training, unemployment, and lack of opportunity.

Americans must understand that none of us will have justice until our legal system becomes truly color blind. Americans will not have peace until all races have equal access to employment, financial opportunities, and economical growth. Each of us has a responsibility to address inequities in our legal, social, and economic system. Whites, Hispanics, and Asians and other racial and ethnic groups must not see all blacks as threats to them or their business. They must not judge all African Americans based on the actions of a small segment of their race. They must stop this type of stereotyping and discrimination. They must not punish all blacks for the L.A. riots. Instead we must acknowledge that all races are capable of vicious attacks on themselves and others. African Americans do not have a monopoly on violence and must not be treated as if they do. This is an example of how all blacks are stereotyped as vicious and hostile.

There is no denying that American society has brutalized blacks and denied justice from the time of slavery (1619) up to the civil rights protests of the sixties. But most non-minorities do deny that these conditions still exist today. They believe new laws and policies have eliminated the inequities of earlier times. They overlook and ignore common unthinkable attacks against African Americans which occur only because of their color. These happen on a daily basis, but the news media rarely reports them unless they are of a sensational nature.

Few people know of the brutal assault on Christopher Wilson, an African-American clerk from Brooklyn, New York, who never missed a day of work. While visiting friends in Tampa, Florida, on New Years Day, 1993, he was abducted at gun point by three white men as he purchased a newspaper. He was forced to drive to a deserted field. There they dosed him with gasoline and set him on fire. As Christopher screamed in pain and struggled for his life, two of the assailants laughed as they walked away. They left behind a note: "One less nigger more to go," signed the KKK. Christopher miraculously survived but received second-degree burns on more than 40 percent of his body. He will be scarred and live in pain for the rest of his life. They caught the three individuals responsible for this horrific act. During the trial one defendant testified they did it to have some fun.

Our justice system showed a lack of concern for Christopher Wilson. The legal authorities allowed a former judge who had not tried a case in more than 20 years to act as chief prosecutor. The former judge made critical and careless mistakes. This almost resulted in the defendants' acquittal. Jurors stated they were only able to find the defendants guilty because Christopher Wilson had identified the defendants. This happened even with one of the three defendants testifying against the other two. The jurors said the prosecutor appeared confused and did not know what he was doing during the trial. One assistant prosecutor resigned because of his poor performance. The verdict was being appealed because of some technical errors made by the chief prosecutor. Receiving inadequate counsel when they are represented in court is common for minorities.

Another recent example of brutality against blacks is the murder in 1992 of 35-year-old Malice Wayne Green. He was beaten to death with fists and flashlights by three Detroit police officers. It occurred when he refused to open his clenched fist after the police had pulled him over. A paramedic testified that Green only had a piece of paper in his hand.

Society must address the issues that cause unjustified police beatings, riots, and racially motivated attacks. Only by doing this can we prevent them from occurring again. Again, these issues are poverty, lack of jobs, inadequate education, high unemployment, discrimination, and the lack of equal justice. Large segments of the black population go to bed hungry every night.

> "Hungry people cannot be good at learning or producing anything, except perhaps violence."
> — Pearl Bailey, Pearl's Kitchen

The shortages of jobs and employment opportunities for minorities are contributors to the social problems in this country. We can make major progress in correcting our social problems by providing jobs. Good jobs are the only cures for poverty. Leaders in the public and private sectors must make major attitude changes and reevaluate their priorities. It starts with objective thinking combined with rational actions. Our nation must stop spending its time and energy focusing on anger and hatred because of the L.A. riots and other similar incidents. This only perpetuates hatred, racism, and discrimination.

Out of every negative situation there is some good. If we must think about the L.A. riots, we should not overlook the positive things that occurred. Neighbors and strangers reached out to help others during and after the riots. They helped others regardless of their race or nationality. Do not allow bigotry to make you view all blacks as heartless human beings. Instead reflect on the heroism and compassion many blacks displayed during the riots. Most people have forgotten how ordinary unarmed African-American men and women risked their lives to save whites, Hispanics, and Asians during the riots.

It is a sad commentary on our society that few of us recall that four African Americans left the safety of their homes to rescue Reginald Denny. They did this because the Los Angeles police withdrew from the area. Without their heroic deeds Reginald Denny would have died. It is because of the courage of Terri Barnett, Lei Yullie, Titus Murphy and trucker Bobby Green that Reginald Denny was saved. None of them knew or had ever met Reginald Denny prior to rescuing him. Titus Murphy and Terri Barnett watched the live coverage of Denny being assaulted on television and came to his rescue. Lei Yullie and Bobby Green did not know each other prior to the rescue. They also witnessed the assault on television and came to Denny's aid.

Lei Yullie was the first to arrive, Murphy and Barnett second, and Bobby Green arrived last. At the scene they knew they had to get Denny immediately to the hospital or he would die. Yullie did what she could to comfort Denny as Bobby Green drove Denny's truck to the hospital. Terri Barnett drove her car in front of the truck to clear a path. Murphy rode on the truck's running board. It did not matter to them that Denny was white and they did not know him. It only mattered that Reginald Denny was a human being who needed help.

During the riots other African Americans risked their lives to save non-black victims. This was the case of Benny Newton, a black minister who risked his life to save a stranger. Fidel Lopez, a Hispanic, was being severely beaten. Benny Newton came to his aid. He shielded Lopez with his body. He told rioters if they were going to kill this man they would have to kill him first. His actions saved Fidel Lopez. Gregory Alan Williams, a black actor in the popular TV series *Baywatch,* went to the intersection of Normandy and Florence during the riots. He went to try to stop the attacks on innocent people. He risked his life to save Taka Hirata, an Asian print shop owner who was being attacked and robbed. Countless other unnamed African Americans went unacknowledged for risking their lives to save non-black victims during the riots. The public news media failed to properly cover these stories.

Whites and other minorities must not overlook the brave and unselfish deeds of African Americans during the L.A. riots. They are testaments that not all blacks hate or want to harm whites and other minorities. This is a clear demonstration that blacks respect the rights of others. This shows that we must judge blacks as individuals and not as a group.

While we are talking about ordinary people who were heroes of the L.A. riot we must not forget Reginald Denny. Reginald did not allow this horrible experience to cause him to hate his attackers or blacks. In fact, immediately after his testimony at the trial of his attackers, Reginald hugged one of his attackers" mothers. He wished her and her family well as he left the court. Forgiveness is an important gesture that starts the healing process between minorities and non-minorities. Reginald Denny showed extraordinary compassion, forgiveness, and humanity. He never tried to spread hatred, nor seek revenge against his attackers or other African Americans. Reginald Denny and other heroes of the L.A. riots showed extraordinary inner strength, courage, and wisdom to put aside the past and work toward a positive future. They set important examples of what we all must strive for, regardless of our race.

Many quotations used in this book describing job discrimination and other racial issues were made more then a hundred years ago. They are as relevant today as when civil rights leaders, elected officials and legal authorities first said them. These problems are not new nor unknown to us. The riots which occurred after the Rodney King verdict should not have surprised anyone. The Rodney King verdict was not what caused the riots on April 29, 1992, in Los Angeles — it was just the breaking point that ignited them.

History always repeats itself under identical circumstances. Twenty-nine years ago (July 28, 1967) after the black civil unrest occurred throughout our nation, President Lyndon B. Johnson established the National Advisory Commission on Civil Disorders. The commission was directed to answers three questions:

- What happened?

- Why did it happen?

- What can be done to prevent it from happening again?

In the same year (1967) and prior to the completion of the report, in his Address to the Nation, President Johnson stated:

> The only genuine, long-range solution for what has happened lies in an attack — mounted at every level — upon the conditions that breed despair and violence. All of us know what these conditions are: Ignorance, discrimination, slums, poverty, disease, not enough jobs. We should attack these conditions — not because we are frightened by conflict, but because we are fired by conscience. We should attack them because there is simply no other way to achieve a decent and orderly society in America.

The following year (1968), the National Advisory Commission on Civil Disorder released their fact-finding report. It was entitled "The Report of the National Advisory Commission on Civil Disorders" and is also known as the Kerner Report. This extensive study reported more than 150 riots or major disorders between 1965 and 1968. It also identified 12 prominent grievances of African Americans. The second most common grievance was unemployment and underemployment and the fourth was inferior education. In 1996, (29 years later) they still list these two issues within the top four grievances of African Americans. Another significant finding stated in the report was, "What White Americans have never fully understood — but what Negroes can never forget — is that white society is deeply implicated in the ghetto. White institutions created it, white institutions maintain it, and white society condones it."

Disproportionate poverty, high unemployment, violence, crime, and drugs continue to run rampant in black communities. They exist only because our country's important institutions — our government, businesses, educational system, and justice system have failed miserably. An important step to correct the inadequacies in our legal system is to create meaningful laws and appropriate punishment that motivate our institutions to change their attitudes toward minorities. These new laws must be based on equal justice for all.

The American government and judicial system must create an environment where people trust, respect, and honor their laws and authority. They must equally apply the system to all and not just to a selected few. Today, minorities, and even many in the non-minority population, view our corporations, government, and judicial system with contempt, mistrust, and shame. They see our institutions as the source of the problems, as having failed to protect the people they are obligated to serve.

Over the entrance to the Supreme Court of the United States carved in stone is this important statement: "Equal Justice Under the Law." This statement must become more than empty words. It must be a rallying cry to the people we entrust with this responsibility. This principle must be guided by truth, integrity, sound morals, and without hidden agendas. The actions of the representatives of the Supreme Court must never be above the review of the people. Many Supreme Court decisions have been improper and in direct violation of principles they are responsible for protecting. "In 1857 the Dred Scott V. Sanford case of the U. S. Supreme Court placed the authority of the Constitution behind decisions made by the states in the treatment of blacks. The Dred Scott decision was that black Americans, even if free, were not intended to be included under the word citizen as defined in the Declaration of Independence and could, therefore, claim none of the rights and privileges provided for in that document."

Throughout the history of America, discriminatory and racist laws were legal. They were in direct violation of African Americans' civil liberties. These laws exploited black Americans. During slavery the rape of a female slave was not a crime against her; it was an act of trespassing on a slave owner's property. Teaching blacks how to read or write was illegal. During slavery blacks were forbidden to carry arms or meet in groups without the presence of a white. Jim Crow Laws made integration illegal (i.e., housing, public facilities, and employment). Between 1882 and 1938 the recorded number of lynchings of blacks was 3,402. All attempts to pass a federal anti-lynching bill during this period were unsuccessful.

African Americans, other minorities, and women are still victims of the inequities in our legal system. They often view justice as a commodity purchased by the party who has the most money and the best lawyers. Laws established to protect minority rights are biased. Violations are difficult to prove and beyond most people's financial abilities to fight.

To survive, Americans must be willing to change biased attitudes and laws. They have embedded them in many cultures and institutions. America must work to accommodate all and not just a chosen few. If America fails to do this, it will not only cause the destruction of minorities but of the non-minority population as well. The frustrations minorities feel from being treated as less than human beings will have a chilling backlash on the growth, safety, and prosperity of our nation. Instead of keeping minorities out of the mainstream, America must allow them to become an important part of it.

Discriminatory practices against blacks and other minorities have come full circle. It now threatens the future of America. Poor education, rampant discrimination, abject poverty, constant injustice, and long-term unemployment have created a sense of hopelessness in our country. These factors have resulted in the high rate of crime and drug use that has plagued our country. Drugs, crime, poverty, lack of skills, hopelessness and a sense of not belonging have created financial burdens that are strangling our country. In a December 13, 1993, *Business Week* article, "The Economics of Crime," it was reported that those crimes cost America 425 billion dollars a year. This exceeds our country's annual defense budget of 300 billion dollars.

The same *Business Week* article stated it costs $20,000 to $30,000 a year to incarcerate a person. The cost to incarcerate a 25 year old for life was $600,000 to $1,000,000. It would cost a fraction of this expense to educate or provide job training to individuals who are disadvantaged, unskilled, or need to be retrained. Education and job training provide hope and positive alternatives to crimes and drugs. These individuals also become contributors to our society (tax payers, employees, business owners). But this alternative will only work if discrimination are eliminated from our society.

In the book *Black Economics,* Jawanza Kunjufu provides a perfect example of how the United States government perpetuates the poverty cycle for millions of Americans. He shows the cost of paying one unskilled AFDC recipient $500 per month ($6,000 a year) for 40 years. This would cost tax payers $240,000, with no return on their investment. Spending $20,000 to $50,000 to educate or train the same individual to earn $20,000 a year would be more effective. This $20,000 income over 40 years would generate income of $800,000. Using a 25 percent tax rate, these same individuals would generate income taxes of $200,000.

America must be willing to understand the motive behind what it does and says about racism and sexism in our country. Racism is so deeply embedded in our society that we routinely engage in it even when it is unintentional. So-called innocent comments and actions hurt regardless if they are unintentional. This fact hit home on the final day of the 1997 Masters Golf

Tournament when long-time golf pro Fuzzy Zoeller made racial comments about Tiger Woods winning the tournament. The winner of the tournament is allowed select the menu for the participants. Near the conclusion of the tournament Fuzzy said, "That little boy [Tiger Woods] is driving well and he's putting well. He's doing everything it takes to win. So, you know what you guys do when he gets in here? You pat him on the back and say, congratulations and enjoy it and tell him not to serve fried chicken next year. Got it? Or collard greens or whatever the hell they serve." While most believe Fuzzy Zoeller meant no real harm, these are harmful and insensitive comments. They are a clear indication how society views African Americans. While Tiger Woods was winning this Master Tournament he broke most of the existing records. Yet he was still viewed in terms of "collard greens and fried chicken," regardless of his accomplishments. Comments like these have a negative impact on African Americans and the way they are viewed and treated in our society. They have a way of belittling and devaluing our accomplishments.

This incident was minor compared to the 1996 revelations that senior executives at Texaco Oil, the nation's third- largest oil company, had plotted to destroy evidence disclosing disparaging racial remarks that were taped during meetings discussing an ongoing discrimination law suit brought by black employees. On tape they discussed altering and destroying records to prevent black plaintiffs from obtaining them. They also referred to African Americans as "jelly beans." Richard A. Lundwall, a senior personnel manager in Texaco's finance department, was heard to state how funny it seemed that "all black jelly beans seem to be glued to the bottom of the bag." He turned over the tapes because he had been terminated. While Texaco did the right thing — acknowledged executives did wrong, settled the pending discriminatory suit for 176 million dollars, and agreed to made important changes — this case is highly unusual because of the discovered tapes. Without the discovery of the tapes, discrimination may never have been proved.

These are not isolated incidents. Other major U.S. corporations and institutions are under fire and facing legal actions for racial and sexual discrimination. Avis Rent-A-Car, the nation's second largest car rental agency, is facing numerous discrimination law suits from African Americans, Orthodox Jews, the ACLU, and others. Three African-American females filed suit against a North Carolina Avis franchise in 1996 for discriminatory practices. This suit was followed by a similar one in 1997 by the

Pennsylvania attorney general's office after an undercover investigation. The attorney general discovered that Avis offices in Harrisburg rented white undercover officers cars after informing African-American customers no cars were available. Avis employees also questioned African Americans and Hispanics more rigorously than Caucasians. They also required African Americans to rent cars for three days, while Caucasians were permitted to rent them for a single day. Another discriminatory lawsuit was filed in 1997 against Avis Tulsa, Oklahoma, for refusing to rent cars to ultra-Orthodox Jews and for using discriminatory language to describe them.

Because of racially discriminatory practices, Denny's Restaurant in 1994 were forced to pay $46 million dollars to black patrons who were victims of discrimination. This suit was filed after six black Secret Service agents guarding President Clinton were unable to get breakfast in a Denny's in Maryland while their white colleagues were served. Part of the settlement required that Denny's retrain employees, feature minorities in ads and open their franchises to them. In 1993 only one of Denny's 168 franchised restaurants was owned by African Americans. In 1998, 32 franchised restaurants are owned by African Americans. In 1998 Denny's suspended a Miami store manager for allegedly refusing to serve a group of prison officers that included blacks, and saying something like, "you guys don't look right together."

One of the largest sexual harassment and abuse complaints was filed by the Equal Employment Opportunity Commission in 1996 against Mitsubishi Motors. The EEOC complaint alleges that 300 to 500 women have been verbally harassed and physically assaulted by co-workers and supervisors, in addition to the 29 women who have sexual-harassment complaints pending in civil court. After massive boycotts and public outcries, in 1997 Mitsubishi has offered to rehire women involved in litigation and invest over $200 million in salaries, services, and products to communities of color and woman-owned businesses.

Astra USA, a unit of Swedish pharmaceutical giant Astra AB, reached a settlement in February 1997 with the EEOC. They agreed to pay $10 million to at least 80 female employees who were sexually harassed by 30 or more men that included senior executives. This agreement was the largest settlement for sexual harassment in the federal agency's history. James Lee, the EEOC lawyer, stated, "It was an atmosphere fostered by the president of the company, and other people followed suit, from managers to customers to guests at social functions from abroad."

Recent revelations abut U.S. military sex scandals have dominated the news. In 1991 it was the Tailhook Navy convention scandal. In 1997 in Aberdeen, Maryland, four drill sergeants and a captain were charged with raping or sexually harassing at least a dozen female recruits. In the same year a national military hotline was established to hear sexual-misconduct complaints. They received thousands of calls. While an extensive new Defense Department survey shows there is a significant reduction in military women reporting sexual harassment, it showed a decrease from 64 percent to 55 percent, which is still unacceptable. While this may sound shocking, sexual harassment had been an accepted practice in the military until recent public outcries.

Anyone who believes that there is a need to end affirmative action needs to review these stories and the thousands more that are not so public. Most businesses and institutions that participate in discrimination or engage in sexual harassment are unwilling to acknowledge it or take actions to prevent them unless they are forced to. This is why we need strong affirmative action laws to protect minorities' and women's rights

I began this book with a memorial to my father. Please read it once more before you set this book down. I feel it is my most powerful indictment of discrimination and the damage it does to the human spirit. I hope this book will be an inspiration to African Americans, other minorities and women. May it inspire all to accept the responsibility to combat discrimination whenever they encounter it. We cannot afford to wait for others to eliminate this problem. Each of us must lead the fight to eradicate these evils. I hope this book teaches its readers to do this in a productive manner. I hope it will be a wake-up call for American businesses, our government and other institutions. I hope this book provides them with valuable insights about the hardships they inflict upon minority employees, citizens and themselves when they promote or ignore discrimination and racism within their organizations. It is my desire that this book will teach American businesses and other institutions that progressively working to eliminate discrimination is not just the right thing to do, it is a matter of their survival and the future survival of our country.

I look forward to the day when Martin Luther King's dream becomes a reality:

"I have a dream my four little children will one day live in a nation where they will not be judged by the color of their skin but by the content of their character. I have a dream today."

This will transform all my suffering and sacrifices into total jubilation.

REFERENCES

Akbar, Na'im. *Visions for Black Men.* Tallahassee, FL: Mind Productions and Associations, 1991.

Bell, Janet Cheatham. *Famous Black Quotations and Some Not So Famous.* Chicago: Sabayt Publications, 1986.

Chessler, Sey, Andrew Hacker, Bill Adler, Anthony DeCurtis, and Jonathan van Meter. "White Men On Black Power." *Essence.* November 1992 (11th Annual Men's issue), pp. 66-70, 124.

Dickens, Floyd, Jr., and Jacqueline B. Dickens. *The Black Manager: Making it in the Corporate World.* New York: Amacom — American Management Association, 1982.

Greenhaus, Jeffrey H., Saroj Parasurman, and Wayne M. Wormey. "Effects of Race on Organizational Experiences, Job Performance Evaluations, and Careers Outcomes," *Academy of Management Journal* 33, no. 1 (March 1990): 64-86.

Hacker, Andrew. *Two Nations, Black and White, Separate, Hostile, Unequal.* New York: Ballantine Books, 1992.

Jamison, Charles W., Jr. "Racism: The Hurt that Men Won't Name." *Essence.* November 1992 (11th Annual Men's issue), pp. 62-64.

Keets, Heather, John Filiatreau, Eric Sokine, James E. Eltie, Paula Dwyer, and Howard Gleckman. "Race in the Workplace: Does Affirmative Action Work?" *Business Week* .8 July 1991, pp. 50-63.

The Kerner Report: The 1968 Report of the National Advisory Commission on Civil Disorders. New York: Pantheon Books, 1968. Out of print.

Kunjufu, Jawanza. *Black Economics.* Chicago: African American Images, 1991.

Mabry, Marcus, Frank Washington, Nadine Joseph, and Howard Manly. "Past Tokenism." *Newsweek* 14 May 1990, p. 37.

Mandel, Michael J., Paul Magnusson, James E. Ellis, Gail DeGeorge, Keith L. Alexander. "The Economics of Crime." *Business Week* 13 December 1993, pp. 72-75, 80, 85.

Munroe, Myles. *Becoming a Leader: Anyone Can Do It.* Bakersfield, CA: Pneuma Life, 1993.

Munroe, Myles. *Releasing Your Potential.* Shippensburg, PA: Destiny
Imaged, 1992.

National Association of Manufacturers. *Report on Manufacturers, 1992.*
Washington: National Association of Manufacturers, 1992.

National Urban League Inc. *The State of Black America* New York: The
National Urban League Inc. Published annually.

*Opportunity 2000: Creative Affirmative Action Strategies for a Changing
Workforce.* Washington: Superintendent of Documents, U.S.
Government Printing Office, 1988.

Pipelines of Progress: A Status Report on the Glass Ceiling. Washington:
Superintendent of Documents, U.S. Government Printing Office,
August 1992.

Sharpe, Rochelle. "Losing Ground: In Latest Recession Only Blacks
Suffered Net Employment Loss." *Wall Street Journal* 14 September 1993,
Section A, pp. 1, 14, 15.

United States Department of Commerce, Economics and Statistics —
Bureau of the Census. *Statistical Abstract of the United States, 1992 : The
National Data Bank.*

United States Department of Labor. *A Report on the Glass Ceiling Initiative.*
Washington: Superintendent of Documents, U.S. Government Printing
Office, August 1991.

Williams, Annette. "When Downsizing Hits Home." *Black Enterprise*
March 1994, pp. 52-59.

*Workforce 2000 — Work and Workers for the 21st Century — Executive
Summary.* Washington, D.C.: Superintendent of Documents, U.S.
Government Printing Office, 1987.

RECOMMENDED READING

Jamieson, David, and Julie O'Mara. *Managing Workforce 2000: Gaining the
Diversity Advantage.* Jossey-Bass, 1991. Price: $27.95

King, Martin Luther, Jr. *A Testament of Hope: The Essential Writings and
Speeches of Martin Luther King, Jr.* San Francisco: Harper San Francisco,
1986. Price: $16.96

"Korn/Ferry's Executive Profile 1990: A Survey of Corporate Leaders, 1990."

Korn/Ferry International Executive Search Firm
237 Park Ave 11th Floor
New York, New York 10017
(212) 687-1834
Attn. Corporate Communications
Price $50.00

"No frills" Diversity Library
ODT Inc.
Box 134 Amherst, Mass 01004
(413) 549-1293. Price $125.00
Library includes 3 books, 1 audio tape, assessment tools, reference list and
other tools.

Morrison, Ann M. *The New Leaders: Guidelines on Leadership Diversity in
America.* Jossey-Bass, 1992. Price: $29.95
Rosener, Loden, and Rosener, Judy B. *Workforce America! Managing
Employee Diversity as a Vital Resource.* One Irwin, 1991. Price: $29.95
Thiederman, Sondra. *Profiting in America's Multi Cultural Marketplace:
How to Do Business Across Cultural Lines.* Lexington Books, 1991. Price:
$24.95
Thomas, Roosevelt, Jr. *Beyond Race and Gender: Unleashing the Power of
Your Total Work Force by Managing Diversity in America.* New York:
AMACOM, 1991. Price: $15.95

NEWSLETTERS AND PUBLICATIONS

Cultural Diversity at Work
13751 Lake City Way N.E., Suite 106
Seattle Wash. 98125-3615
Price $64.00 (six issues and 11 bulletins)

How to Recruit Older Workers (D13279)
How to Manager Older Workers (D13288)
How to Train Older Workers (D13287)

(When ordering include title and stock number)
Joan Kelly
Business Partnerships, American Association of Retired Persons:
601 E Street N.W.
Washington, D. C. 20049
(202) 434-2092

Managing Diversity
P.O. Box 819
Jamestown, N.Y. 14702-0819
1-899-542-7869
Price $79.50 (12 issues)

VIDEOS AND FILMS

Bridging Cultural Barriers: Managing Ethnic Diversity in the Workplace
Barr Films
12801 Schabarum Ave.
Irwindale, Calif. 91706-7878
1 800 234-7878
A training tape for managers and supervisors (10% discount if you mention Nation's Business)

Valuing Diversity
Griggs Productions
302 23rd Ave.
San Francisco, Calif. 94121
(415) 668-4200
This seven-part film can be rented or purchased

OTHER RESOURCES

National Conference of Black Mayors, Inc.
1422 West Peachtree Street N.W., Suite 800
Atlanta, GA 30309
Phone (404) 892-0127
Fax (404) 876-4597
web site http://www.rtk.net/blackmayors.html

Bureau of Labor Statistics
http://www.bls.gov

Labor Force Statistics from Current Populations Survey
http://www.stats.bls.gov

Labor Force Statistics
(202) 606 6378
http://stats.bls.gov/cpshome

Howard University Web Site
http://www.howard.edu

Affirmative Action and Diversity Project: A Web Page for Research
http://humanitas.ucsb.edu/projects/aa/aa.html
http://humanitas.ucsb.edu/projects/aa/pages/Prop-209.html
Also lists other affirmative action web pages.

The Glass Ceiling Commission
US Department of Labor
Office of Public Affairs
Washington DC
Contact Diane Quinn (202) 219 5502 or
Gordon Berg (202) 219 7342
http://www.ilr.cornell.edu

INDEX

CBC. *See* Congressional Black Caucus.
Civil Rights Acts, 81-82
class action suits, 139
Clinton, Bill, 101-102
complainants, 54
Congressional Black Caucus (CBC), 98-99, 102
Connerly, Ward, 145
consultants, use of for anti-discrimination training, 150
crime, cost of, 176

D

day care, 161
degrading comments, 35-36, 177
Denny's Restaurant, 177
Denny, Reginald, 169
Department of Fair Employment and Housing (DFE&H), 42, 141-143, 145, 154
DFE&H. *See* Department of Fair Employment and Housing.
discrimination
       complaints about, 60, 126
       definition of, 137
       See Also access discrimination; reverse discrimination;
       treatment discrimination.
discriminatory patterns, 39, 40
diversity, 69, 71-72, 147
downsizing, 41, 47

E

EEOC. *See* Equal Employment Opportunity Commission.
Equal Employment Opportunity Commission (EEOC), 42, 74, 82, 85, 141-143, 154, 178
ethics, 150-151